HOW TO MANAGE YOURSELF

HOW TO MANAGE YOURSELF

(Revised and Updated)

By Med Serif

Frederick Fell Publishers, Inc.
New York, N.Y.

For information address:

Frederick Fell Publishers, Inc.
386 Park Avenue South
New York, New York 10016

Library of Congress Catalog Card Number: 81-1555
International Standard Book Number: 0-8119-0425-3

Printed and Bound in Canada
1 2 3 4 5 6 7 8 9 0

Marilyn,
this book is dedicated
to you alone.

How to Succeed in Business by Trying

In mid-1958, a fascinating new frontier was opened for me by L. T. White, then vice president of Cities Service Petroleum, a subsidiary of the Cities Service Company. L. T. was, you could say, pioneering in a vast new area—big business assistance to small business.

Working with him to do more than offer just the normal advertising, promotion, and accounting assistance, we sought to help men and women improve their managerial abilities.

In our research, we soon saw that even the best executive could easily become completely tied up in a mass of detail. The performance of the modern executive—whether owner, hired manager, or employee—is the cornerstone for the success of a business in our highly competitive society. Too many men and women fail to achieve complete success because they do not operate at the fullest efficiency at all times.

Believing that executives could grow in ability by learning to be more effective, we began trying to help them do a better job of self-management. We wrote articles, prepared booklets, gave speeches, and taught classes. Our findings proved of equal value and interest to the owners of businesses and to the executives of large and small companies.

This is a field which seems to have no end. Every time I talk to someone, new subjects are suggested. Basically, however, they all fall into three specific areas—improving self-efficiency, human relations with others, and living a fuller personal life.

In this book I've tried to answer many of the questions and to offer solutions to problems that are faced by busy men and women. I offer thanks to Cities Service for both the opportunity to explore this fascinating field and for permission to utilize some of our research in the writing of this book.

MED SERIF

Contents

Your Personal Life

MANAGING
YOURSELF

1
The MAN or WOMAN
in Management

How often have you felt there just weren't enough hours in the day to meet all the demands your business or your job makes of you? I doubt that Congress will ever legislate a 28-hour day into existence, so it's up to you to become more effective in your everyday work.

In today's tightly competitive business world this is especially true. Success comes to the organization which is just a little bit better than its competition. In most cases that slight edge lies not in machinery, or even products. It lies in the men and women running the business.

Modern medicine hasn't yet found a pill that will make you a better "self"-manager. But there are things you can do. In a large sense, this book will point out objectives and methods for reaching the peak in self-efficiency.

There Is a Secret

Successful men and women have found the secret of "getting on top of their jobs." Their secret, if you want to call it that, is threefold:

1. You must want to work at top efficiency.
2. You must organize yourself.
3. Once you've stopped "spinning your wheels," you must discipline yourself to stick to your new-found efficiency.

An executive's job is basic. You must see opportunity. You must plan. You must organize. You must control. You must improve and change course whenever necessary.

The ease and speed with which you accomplish these tasks depend upon a combination of factors, basically all within you. Your succeess is based on your innate abilities, your acquired skills, your efficiency, health and vigor, your foresight, and your desire to succeed.

No matter what your job or your business, you are probably well organized to meet mechanical breakdowns or similar headaches. Preventive maintenance would probably have caught any problems at their start. Friction between people or departments is quickly eliminated.

Yet, when it comes to operating at maximum efficiency, we are apt to find the job too often runs us. The answer is simple. Too many managers fail to manage themselves. As a result, they barely limp along at half or less efficiency.

The Briefcase Every Night

The son of a large multistate oil-distributor friend is a perfect example. He told me, "When I took the business over from Dad three years ago, I was able to run it and I still had time for my family, my golf, and the other things we enjoyed. Now, I lug the briefcase home just about every night. Nothing I do seems to help. I never seem to get caught up. What's wrong?"

I spent the next few days following him around his office and his bulk plants. It didn't take long to spot just what had gone wrong.

My friend had left his son a solid enterprise. The boy had learned his lessons well and had added new innovations and equipment. He spent a good deal of time talking to people in the oil and other businesses. He listened to and questioned his suppliers and his bankers. His business flourished.

He gave everything his personal touch. Today, he was still trying to keep his fingers in every pie. The business had more than tripled in size, but he still had only two hands, two feet, two eyes, one brain, and the same twenty-four hours a day he had before.

I bluntly spelled out the trouble as I saw it: "You are wasting too much time on details, and spending too little time actually doing your job—managing."

He readily saw this and agreed. But how was he to become more effective on the job?

Actually he had taken the first step when he admitted that he had tied his hands with red tape and details. He had begun to organize himself. Only self-management would make him more effective in his work.

Managing vs. Operating

The transition from operating a business or a job to managing is a mental one. It's been said there are four steps:

1. Realize that you can't do all the work yourself.
2. Admit that you can't make every decision. You must trust others to make some for you.
3. Recognize the importance of planning.
4. Continually check your progress.

It's not easy to manage yourself. Some of us are too tired to make the effort. Others are indifferent and content to let things just roll along. A few may be too lazy to try. But if you were to weigh the results of self-organization, you would quickly see the solid gold advantages that would fall to you. Here are six of the more prominent:

1. You do more, and what you accomplish is better.
2. You can set goals for yourself.

3. You can continually check to see if you are on course.
4. You can save time.
5. You eliminate habits that bring ulcers and sleepless nights.
6. You do a better job of leading and inspiring others.

Self-Discipline Is the Key

Organization and operating efficiency, like charity, should begin at home. Ask yourself honestly if you are now performing at 100 percent efficiency every minute of your working day. If you are not, the answer is self-discipline. You must decide that you and only you will be boss. Distractions are ruled out. You must see to it that you complete your work in the fastest possible time, without any wasted energy.

Good planning starts with the formulation of a schedule. Keep a careful record of your activities over a period of several weeks. Be sure to note the jobs you've failed to find time for, as well as those you've completed.

Chapter 2 will fully discuss the management of time and tell you how to analyze your time. For our purposes here, we should emphasize that a careful analysis of your working time is essential. It will reveal that certain activities are probably done on a regular basis. Others happen only occasionally. One suggestion is to group your different activities according to the people you work with.

A second suggestion is to group your tasks according to the nature of the work. Similar activities should be linked up. Your work on one project may be useful on another job. For example, planning and decision-making could be done right after the morning mail is read. Or you might hold them for next to the last thing, until just before you consider your next day's activities.

In a nutshell, your different tasks should fall into a logical order, based on their relative importance. With first preference given to important jobs, the routine will be taken care of during spare time.

Many successful executives handle these routine jobs during their spare time. It is amazing how much time can be wasted traveling to or from work, waiting to see clients, or sitting at your desk waiting for a late caller. This is the time to look over papers, to sign mail, to read your business publications.

Deferred business must be scheduled ahead, and some tool, such as a "tickler" file, must be used to call it to mind in plenty of time for careful thought and action. A tool I've found helpful is a handy booklet that provides spaces for the following data: date job acknowledged; job description; date job is due; date job completed, or dropped, or transferred. Another valuable item, especially in these days of close tax accounting, is a spiral-bound calendar book. Get one that lists every day of the month. List your appointments on each day, and also special projects handled. This becomes an excellent diary of your activities throughout the year.

In all this talk of planning, care should be taken to allow for the handling of any emergencies or problems that might arise.

In Chapter 2 we'll see how to break up your day into time-work blocks. You simply set up a schedule and manage yourself so that you stick to this schedule. A major advantage of such a schedule is that it points out poor use of time.

The "Too Busy" Bosses

Killing the working day seems to be the favorite hobby of many executives at all levels. Some years ago the U.S. Small Business Administration (SBA) identified some of these "busy, busy bosses." They were called:

The Detail-Hugger: Hardly a day passes without his presence distracting the mailroom clerk ("Have you got enough stamps?"), the secretaries ("How do you put a new ribbon on that new machine?") He is also terribly interested in the amount of string used for packages and the amount of gas used by the company trucks.

The Conference Caller: This type won't let anyone order a dozen paper cups without the trappings of a time-killing executive summit meeting. He likes to hear his own voice, even if no one else does.

The Dream Merchant: He kills time dreaming (and worse luck, talking) about what he's going to do tomorrow, and so he never has time to do anything today.

The Kibitzer: Killing his day is not a problem. He just does it by looking over everybody's shoulder, and dropping in on departments "Just to see how things are going."

The One-Track Manager: Charlie-One-Track loves business statistics. Figures fascinate him, and he spends the day poring over them, while decisions that have to be made just wait.

The Overflowing-Desk Man: Killing the day is no problem for this man. He wastes time signing innumerable notes, memos, requisitions and other interoffice trivia.

The Genius: He knows everybody's job so much better than the man doing it that he spends most of his time managing everyone's time and effort . . . but never his own.

The Open Door Man: "My door (this executive announces proudly) is open to everybody at all times." The idea is fine, but the result is disastrous. His employees take up most of his day with trivial questions that they could figure out for themselves if the boss hadn't given them a green light to kill his day.

Naturally, not all men and women fall into one or another of these categories. The really successful ones spend their time managing, controlling, planning and directing the work of others.

Stick to Your Schedule

Once you have analyzed what must be done and prepared a schedule, you must stick to this plan of organization. Everything should be completed in the time period allotted. This schedule serves three purposes:

1. It assures that a job will be completed in the allotted time with the desired results.
2. It permits you to check your own progress.
3. If you've gone astray, you'll know where and when, and you can take the necessary action.

What's Actually Your Job

You can help organize yourself if you carefully reappraise what is actually expected of you. The SBA suggests that many men and women could better organize themselves if they were to follow this simple blueprint for executive thought and action:

1. **Realize that your business, or any business, becomes more complex as it grows.**
    It may require the skills and abilities of such experts as accountants, lawyers, or management consultants, as well as the capable people in your own organization.
2. **Realize that your job is to see your business as a whole.**
    The job of these hired and salaried experts is to provide special knowledge.
3. **Your function is to supply top policy.**
4. **Your purpose is to lead, inspire, direct.**
5. **Never stop reevaluating your job.**
    Ask yourself daily whether you are doing all you should. Are you neglecting some other tasks, or doing some that should better be left to others?
6. **Each day set aside some time to think.**
    Close your door and make sure no one interrupts you. Take all the time you need. On some days it may only be a few minutes. Other days may require hours.
7. **Each day set aside some time to make plans for the future.**
8. **Each day make certain that you have taken care of the important things before you tackle anything else.**

9. Each day be sure to do all the tasks you should be doing, even the unpleasant ones.

Perhaps the paper work is unpleasant and you'd rather be talking to a favorite customer. To do things you dislike means that you have disciplined yourself.

10. Each day do some "on-the-job" coaching.

That means training your assistants to help you and to do their own jobs at a better level of efficiency.

11. Each day remember that you are working with friends.

A smile and a pleasant word can often accomplish the impossible.

12. At the end of each day sit back and think about the tasks you worked on.

Ask yourself if you could have left some undone and completed others. Were there important tasks left undone? Was time wasted on pleasant work while less appealing, but more important, jobs were left undone?

To sum it all up, only organization can put you on the road to complete efficiency and job satisfaction. With organization, you know what goals you want to reach and, with careful thought, just how you are going to get there.

The first steps for self-organization are the ones we will describe later in this book to help us make decisions. They are:

1. Clearly define your problem. In this case it is organizing to meet a specific problem.
2. Carefully analyze all pertinent aspects of the problem.
3. Develop alternative solutions for the problem.
4. Select the one best solution.
5. Translate your decision into action.

We need add only a schedule to be adhered to, and the management action of changing course if our first solution proves unsuitable, to have a comprehensive plan for self-management.

Use All Available Aids

Self-management demands more than just a carefully planned schedule. You must make the fullest use of all available tools at your disposal. These include your own body, your mind, and a variety of physical equipment.

Today's business world exacts a heavy toll of our nervous systems and our bodies. Later in this book we'll discuss working under tension and maintaining your health.

There are too many ways to waste your valuable energy. You can waste a substantial amount of time by acquiring poor habits of concentration, planning, or even thinking.

You can waste your time because you've let bad eating and sleeping habits drain your energy. Failure to control emotions handcuffs many men and women. The failure to use properly the tools at hand, such as the telephone or your desk, also cause you to waste time.

There is a way to stop these energy leaks. It is the self-discipline already mentioned. You must decide that you will be boss, and that you want to complete your work in the fastest time, without wasted energy.

Your mind is the most important asset you have in achieving self-organization. It can be made an important ally if you try to concentrate on improving three areas of your mental activities:

1. **Improve your ability to concentrate.**
      One tip: Keep distractions to a minimum.
2. **Continually increase your knowledge so you can more readily analyze ideas and problems and make the right decision.**
3. **Your memory is a muscle.**
      Exercise it so you are able to retain and recall information when it is needed.

Each of these mental abilities can be developed to the highest degree. Watch others work. Analyze your own working habits. Study and hold fast to the desire to improve. Make resolutions to overcome bad habits, and see that you keep these resolutions. You can replace bad habits with good ones because all patterns of behavior have to be learned, and you can guide and control your learning.

The Physical Aids

Beyond your mind and your body there are certain physical tools to use. Let's start simply. How many of you carry a pencil and a small note pad? Don't trust your memory. Write everything down. The facts or figures you forget can spell the difference between profit and loss.

When I first began to travel as a business magazine editor some years ago, it seemed easy to remember all requests that were made of me. After several years and many conventions, I sat down at my desk on a Monday morning after one convention and looked at the cards I had collected. Each represented a request. But who wanted reprints? Who had asked me to make a convention speech? Which operation had the makings of a good feature article? My mind was a complete blank.

Since that day I've always taken notes. Perhaps too many notes, but when I make a promise, I know I'll fulfill it.

Time is definitely essential for following a schedule. It may seem silly to say this, but own and carry a good watch.

An efficient office and desk are other important aids to the busy executive. They are your base of operation. They can save time and steps and speed the flow of work. Both your desk and office require careful planning. Pull out any drawer in your desk. Is it really organized, or do you have to shuffle through an assortment of cards, papers, envelopes, and paper clips?

Here are three rules for efficient office and desk organization:

1. Locate the most used furniture and equipment as close as possible.

If you do a lot of figuring, have a calculator in your office. Don't force yourself to walk out to find one that someone else may be using.

2. Make the office as attractive as possible, but do not let it distract you.

Colors should be restful and cheerful. Pictures should be of your choice but should fit into the overall scheme.

3. Your desk should hold only immediately usable work and necessary supplies.

Papers belong in their proper files. Reminders such as addresses, phone numbers, and other similar information may be kept either in a box on your desk or in a drawer.

The human element in the office may be the most important. When you've arrived at the level to either share a secretary or to have your own, that person should be carefully trained. It will be this individual's responsibility to protect you from unnecessary callers, to remind you of pending projects, and to do a million other things. We'll discuss more completely the role of this vital person in Chapter 5.

Getting on top of your job will help you accomplish your work in far fewer hours and in a more accurate and efficient manner. It will assure you that you are making the fullest use of your God-given talents. When you achieve this pinnacle, success will have more than monetary value. You will have achieved a sense of tremendous satisfaction for a job well done.

2
How to Manage Your Time

Successful men and women have learned how to make time work for them. They have also proved that others can learn how to make the most out of each working day.

When you achieve this peak, you need no longer fear those Friday or Saturday afternoons that used to close out a week—with a pile of work left undone. Time has become your servant. No longer are you a time-killer.

There are four steps to taking full control of the all-too-few working hours you have. These steps are:

1. You must measure your time.
2. You must find where you waste time.
3. You must plan the most effective use of your hours.
4. You must continually look for short cuts and ways to save time.

How to Measure Time

Preparation of a timetable calls first for analysis of all of your activities. Here you carefully analyze not only the jobs you've completed, but also those for which you failed to find time.

Looking back you'll quickly find that certain activities are regularly repeated. Others are faced only occasionally. The following Analysis Form will help you prepare a profile of your activities.

Activity	Daily		Weekly							Monthly			
	AM	PM	M	T	W	T	F	S	S	1st Week	2nd Week	3rd Week	4th Week

Each daily activity should be checked in the morning or afternoon period on which it is handled. Weekly jobs should be checked by the day the work is done. Each monthly job should be checked in the week the work is normally done. If an activity is done more than once, check the appropriate squares.

A second method for analyzing time provides an actual measurement of the time spent in each activity. This analysis can be done with a simple sheet of ruled paper. Start by putting the hour you begin work on the top line at the left. On the second line put the next quarter hour. On the third line the next quarter hour, etc., continuing until you reach the end of your working day. For example, if you start at 8 A.M., put that on the top line; 8:15 on the second line, and so on.

Now draw lines down the page. This separates the sheet into columns. Write at the top of each column the things you do. For instance, you might write at the head of one column "Reading Mail." "Dictation" might head a second column. A third could be "Visiting Customers." List everything that your job entails.

Activities

Time	READING MAIL	DICTATION	SALES CALLS	WRITING REPORTS	SALES MEETINGS	WAITING	TRAVEL
8:00							
8:15							
8:30							
etc.							

When you have the form made, sit down at the end of the first day. Think back through the hours of the day and put checkmarks under the things you did. Go down the page and account for every quarter hour.

When you count the marks in each column, you'll be able to see, at a glance, what proportion of your time was spent at each activity. When you add up the checkmarks, you'll have measured your time.

After you've measured your time, carefully analyze your activities with this thought uppermost in your mind: Am I allocating the proper time to my different tasks? If the unimportant seem to take too much time, rearranging just a few key jobs will often make a tremendous difference in your rate of efficiency.

In other words: work smarter, not harder.

Scheduling Your Time

Each person must find the one best way to manage the use of his or her time. One of the most used and simplest techniques is to sit down on Sunday night and carefully list everything you want to do during the coming week. It is wise to list these projects by day, with the most important tasks heading each daily list.

Keep this list in front of you throughout the week. Every time a job is completed, you've earned the right to scratch it off your list. Those uncompleted jobs will begin to haunt you, as the list sits on your desk or burns a hole in your pocket.

Some men and women prefer to make out their checklists each night for the coming day. Their aim is to complete each day's assigned work before closing the calendar on that day. It becomes a matter of pride to go home with all scheduled work accomplished.

When the checklist is prepared is unimportant. The important thing is to get into the habit of thinking out a schedule.

In Chapter 1 we suggested that you segregate your activities according to importance and link them with other tasks that logically come together. When this is done, you'll often find that information developed, or work you've completed on one project can be utilized as background material for another project.

I saw a personal example of this some time ago. My employer donated my time to the Small Business Administration so that I could prepare a booklet, "Developing an Assistant." The research I did for this project was utilized later when I developed a sales management series as part of our dealer-relations activities. You'll find this material as the basis of Chapter 17.

It is a good rule to try to make one minute do the work of two by utilizing your efforts to produce information or material that can be used in more than one way.

Budgeting Activities

Budgeting your time simply means breaking down your workday into the time you'll spend on each activity. The two simple systems for analyzing time we illustrated earlier in this chapter should help you do this.

There are just two ways to make the most of your time. One is to eliminate things that don't have to be done. The other is to work as hard as possible on the essential activities that are left.

Once you've analyzed your workday to separate the essential from the unessential tasks, the next step is to decide which jobs must be given a regular place on your schedule, and which should be handled during a free or open period.

Too many people waste time by doing the jobs they like or find easiest first. This is poor management. The sales manager who sells is not really a manager. He sells simply because he want to get the job done, or because he'd rather do it himself. A good manager or supervisor supresses his other interests and concentrates solely on his job—building a stronger business. He hires workers and delegates the work. Remember, one of the prime rules of management is that the lowest-paid individual qualified to do a job is given the assignment.

Your own analysis will quickly show if the odds and ends and trifles have been eating up your time. Concentrating on the really important work will become a habit. The simple checklist made out once a month or every night will quickly put the spotlight on those essential jobs that must have priority.

How important is it to get rid of the unessentials? Just stop for a moment to see what your wasted time is actually costing you.

When You Earn	Every Hour Costs You	Every Minute Costs You	In One Year, One Wasted Hour Daily Costs You
$15,000	$ 7.68	$ .126	$1,881
20,000	10.24	.168	2,508
25,000	12.80	.210	3,133
30,000	15.36	.253	3,762
40,000	20.49	.336	5,016
50,000	25.60	.420	6,266

*Based on 244 eight-hour work days a year.

So you see, the time you possess is worth a great deal. Don't spend it in foolish pursuits.

Gaining More Time

Is it possible to add more minutes or even hours to a day? The answer is *yes,* if you will use the secret ingredient— management; more specifically, in this case, the management of your time.

The first step is to understand that your time is worth money. The preceding chart emphatically points this out. You must also accept the fact that you can only do a better job when you are willing to make an effort.

The next logical step is to set goals for yourself. You may wish to visit more customers, dictate more letters, read more reports or books, or have more time for your family, or to play golf. You must set goals, and you must make every effort to stay right on the path toward these targets.

One automobile salesman I know is successful because he always has prospects in some stage of being ready to be "closed." His secret is to continually find "hot" new prospects. He makes it his daily business to mail at least five postcards to new names, to make at least five phone calls to those he's already contacted or sold, and to make five personal calls on those just about ready to close.

He does all this while taking his turn on the sales floor. How does he do it? He has set his personal daily goals of five for each category and he keeps a regular score on his desk pad. He has no spare minutes, because when a lull comes along, he is making a phone call, writing a card, or driving off to a demonstration.

Is he a success? Ask his boss.

You can set goals for any task. Some years ago, while working for a business magazine, I was writing my thesis for a master's degree. After spending the five weekdays over a hot typewriter, I did not look forward to writing at night or on weekends.

I finally challenged myself to do five pages a night and twenty pages each Saturday and Sunday until the project was completed. My wife agreed to help. Each night I put five paper clips in a coffee cup on one side of the table. As I finished each page, I took one clip out of the cup. Every so often my wife would stop by to check my progress. When the cup had been emptied of four of the clips, she was to put on the coffee and start to make me a sandwich or cut a piece of pie. The coffee would be poured into the empty cup when the last clip was removed.

The first night my wife gave up and went to bed after waiting an hour past our regular bedtime. The second night I made it, but about thirty minutes late. The third night, I hit my goal with a little time to spare. From then on I hit my goal every night.

Pinpointing Your Goals

It is wise to pinpoint your goals. A lot of people waste time and energy simply because they do not have a clear idea of what they want or are supposed to do.

This is the place where the five-step program for self-organization described in Chapter 1 comes in handy. Before you begin any job, mentally run through the following five steps:

1. Define your problem as clearly as possible.
2. Carefully analyze all pertinent aspects.
3. Develop alternative solutions.
4. Select the one best solution.
5. Translate your decision into action.

Setting Realistic Deadlines

Any timetable you set for yourself should be a realistic one. Before you actually set your deadlines, you must allow yourself sufficient time to gather and analyze all pertinent facts and to contact all others who are involved in the project in any way.

You must also gather any tools or supplies that the job may require. If you don't prepare yourself, you may waste a lot of valuable time stopping to get a fact book, or even paper or a typewriter ribbon.

Allow time for the unexpected. Sickness, emergencies, unexpected visitors, even a loss of energy as the day draws to a close will cause wasteful delays. If the delays fail to occur, you'll look just that much better because you finished the job early.

See if you can beat the deadlines you set. This provides an extra incentive and may actually increase your efficiency. Tests show that the rapid worker is often more accurate than the slower one. This might be because the rapid worker is like an automobile driver. He tries out different speeds of work. When he finds the one at which he is most efficient, he continues along at that pace. The slow worker may never really discover what he can do.

How to Acquire More Time

You can acquire more time. Yes—time, like any other commodity, can be bought, it can be manufactured, and it can even be stored. You can gain time in various ways, so here are some hints:

1. Get up fifteen minutes earlier to avoid the morning rush and also streamline your procedure for getting out of your home.

> You can do this by keeping your personal items grouped together, ready for use. It's also a help to decide the night before what to wear and to have your clothes laid out. You will arrive at work feeling much more relaxed when you eliminate morning fumbling.

2. Increase your reading and writing skills.

> Wouldn't it be wonderful to read all those publications and reports and to have them flow across your desk almost as soon as they arrive? You can learn to increase your reading speed. In like manner, you can learn to write better reports, letters, and memos. You'll see how this is done in Chapters 5 and 14. These skills will save you much time.

3. **Develop the habit of making good notes.**

 Store your ideas, facts, figures, and bits of information. Keep reference files and tickler files to guide
 you in your everyday activities. The good note-taker
 finds that he can drop even the biggest problems and
 come back later to pick up the threads without
 wasting time trying to remember facts.

 Make it a habit to prepare notes, either during or
 immediately after meetings or important conversations. Get the facts and decisions made down on
 paper while they are still fresh in your mind. This
 saves time and avoids misunderstandings.

4. **Be decisive and act fast.**

 This prevents strangulation by the loose ends. For instance, answer your correspondence at once and you
 will be rid of almost 95 percent of it. You can then
 concentrate on the special or creative problems involved in the other 5 percent.

 Some executives I know dictate even though all
 the facts are not yet available. They leave blank spaces
 for their secretaries to insert the needed information
 when it becomes available. If they must leave a loose
 end, they specify who is to do what, when. One big
 advantage here is that you do not have to come back
 to a task and spend a great deal of time refreshing
 your memory.

5. **Control your telephone.**

 This fine invention saves you time-consuming travel.
 Instead of "legging it" down to see somebody, pick
 up the phone. It is a fast way of getting information,
 of checking facts, or for giving instructions.

 But this same telephone can become a monster if
 you allow yourself to be drawn into time-wasting bull
 sessions. Get your spouse out of the habit of calling
 you for every little thing. Generally those worries or
 conversations can wait until you get home. Also cut
 out any nonessential phone calls thay you may have
 gotten into the habit of making.

Before you make a business call, make certain you have everything you need at hand—pencil, note paper, any pertinent data, and the phone number and extension you will be calling.

6. **Keep idle chit-chat under control.**

Purely social conversation is important to building good business and social relationships. It's good for morale and it also helps relax the tension. But it can be easily overdone. A twenty-minute fish story is probably eighteen minutes of waste.

7. **Make use of all spare time.**

Many businesspeople handle the routine jobs during their spare moments. If a scheduled caller fails to appear, don't sit idly, tapping a pencil or biting your nails while you wait for your next appointment to show up. Pick up another job and start on it.

Spend any short unexpected time you have signing mail or reading correspondence or reports. The time waiting to see a customer or prospect can be spent going over material in your briefcase. If you commute to work by train or bus, look through papers or business magazines, or spend your trip thinking. You might also take one or two nights a week at home reading business or other publications.

8. **Keep the work in front of you, the distractions away.**

This is especially true if the task is one that is not particularly exciting. Put those other projects that might be more appealing away and concentrate only on the one job that must be completed.

9. **Don't become bogged down in details.**

You should delegate responsibility to somebody else worth considerably less per hour. This calls for the selection of the employee who can be of the most assistance.

10. **Get the important and hard jobs done first.**

Give the key matters your attention while you are at your peak. Save those "let-down" periods for opening and reading routine correspondence or some similar job. Start the tough jobs first thing in the morning.

11. **Look for short cuts.**

    Here, again, is the place to use an assistant if you have one. It is also wise to experiment. You might find a new time-saving approach.

12. **Keep working conditions pleasant.**

    You'll do more, and at a faster pace, if your surroundings are as comfortable as possible. In general, a temperature of 68–70 degrees, with humidity at 50 percent, is best. Proper lighting is another factor that will ease your work.

13. **Take a break from the tough ones.**

    If a job has you stymied for the moment, back off and come back primed with new solutions.

14. **Stop daydreaming.**

    Don't build up a storehouse of ideas you'll "get around to" doing someday. If an idea is really good, it deserves to be put into action now.

    Each of us is allotted only 24 hours a day. The time we waste is our own. If we make intelligent use of our time, we can be assured of the satisfaction that comes from the success we achieve in our work, and from the added hours we can begin to spend with our loved ones.

3
Are You Becoming Obsolete?

People, just like products and equipment, do become obsolete.

Frightening, isn't it? But it's true and it can happen to each one of us. Fortunately, however, a person can fight back and avoid this advanced case of "mental rust."

This chapter will offer some quick, personal checks for you. It's a bit like taking a reading of your blood pressure and pulse to see how you are physically. Ask yourself the probing questions that follow. Then, if you're not quite pleased with the "readings," you're on the track to a better future. Chapter 4 will provide more ideas to make certain you don't become an antique.

1. **How long has it been since you established personal goals?**
   The person without goals is heading for personal obsolescence. A man or woman with personal goals has already begun planning and thinking about how to achieve them.
2. **Plan ahead, by asking yourself, "Where do I want to be next year, in five years, and in 10 years?"**
   And then, "What must I do to reach these goals?"
3. **Do you understand your company's goals?**
   If you do, then you automatically are up on other things, like the objectives of your business, and where you fit in the scheme of things, and what you must do to be highly rewarded.

4. **Have you developed a managerial philsophy?**

   The development of ideas or values for managing yourself and others requires creative, systematic thinking.

5. **Do you systematically attempt to improve?**

   Do you set goals?

6. **Are you open-minded toward newness?**

   Do you try to avoid a closed mind that will stop you from mastering new techniques or ideas? You should be ready and willing to try something that failed once before.

7. **Do you accept promotions or job changes?**

   They will expose you to new situations and activities and lead to greater awareness and knowledge. Whether it's a lateral shift from department to department, or a vertical move upward, changes mean you are growing on the job.

8. **Do you hire thoughtlessly rather than surrounding yourself with the best people you can find?**

   Remember that the strong manager becomes even stronger by building a strong organization.

9. **Do you attend professional meetings, conferences or seminars?**

   When did you last do so? They are designed to advance your knowledge. If you are told to go, do you immediately start figuring how to avoid attending the business sessions? It is often possible to obtain enough information to complete your report through after-hour bull sessions. But what have you really gained?

10. **Do you avoid reading?**

    Those trade publications, business magazines and scholarly journals are tools to help you avoid becoming obsolete. Don't let your subscription lapse. If the publication is circulated in your office, cross your initials off the routing slip only after you've checked the item over.

Honesty pays. If you have really analyzed yourself, you have taken a good step toward avoiding personal obsolescence. The secret is to think and to learn. The next chapter will show you how to keep learning throughout your life. It's the true prescription to avoid becoming obsolete.

4
Don't Ever Stop Learning

Remember that old notion, "You can't teach an old dog new tricks?" Well, it's just not so.

No matter what your age, you can continue to increase your store of knowledge. This is an extremely important ability today because learning does go hand-in-hand with success. No one need stay in one job because he feels he lacks the capacity to grow. This chapter will show you how you can keep learning in a businesslike manner.

Take a New Look

The first step is to rid yourself of the idea that once you have finished formal schooling, whether at high school or college, your learning is over except for improving your immediate job skills.

Nothing could be further from the truth. Educators tell us that one of the most desirable times to learn is the period between 20 and 40. But you needn't stop there. If you have the desire to learn, there is no reason why you shouldn't be able to learn throughout your life.

There are three simple guideposts to learning:

1. You must want to learn.
2. You must set goals for yourself.
3. You must use every possible technique of learning.

You Had the Desire to Learn

Remember when you were a youngster? If, say, you were a baseball fan, you probably knew the batting average of every member of your favorite baseball team and those of every other leading star. You could probably name the starting lineups for every major league nine.

It was easy to remember these names and numbers because you wanted to. This is the important secret for learning. By pinpointing your reasons for wanting to master whatever knowledge you need, you've given yourself the desire to forge ahead. For example, knowledge of accounting, business law, salesmanship, or some technical skills will help you do a better job. This can lead to promotions, salary increases, and a better life for your family. If you are in business for yourself, the ability to do a better job will assure the success of your enterprise, bringing with it all the rewards you desire.

Setting Your Goals

To learn anything effectively, you must first define your goals. Now sit back and study yourself to see what you can do to help yourself reach your goals.

Ask yourself some questions: What is my goal? What do I feel I must be able to do to reach this goal? Why must I reach this goal? What does reaching my target require in personality factors and in habits? What can I do to help myself reach my goals?

Every target must be a realistic one. Unless it is, you will face unbearable frustration. You *can* learn accounting. You *can* learn to play golf. You *can* learn to operate a piece of machinery. But don't forget: you can learn to swim, but it is certainly unrealistic to expect to swim an ocean, no matter how much you may want to.

Set your goals realistically, looking at both the positive and negative aspects of what you want to learn.

It is important to have confidence in your ability to learn. In your lifetime you've already acquired a tremendous amount of knowledge. The so-called simple skills such as walking, running, and talking were not easy for an infant. Today, you do arithmetic without a second thought, though your checkbook may sometimes not balance. But do you remember all those days from first grade on through high school, and even college, when you never thought you'd be able to understand how to add, subtract, multiply, divide, work with fractions, or be able to do advanced mathematics?

First, Learn How to Learn

Perhaps the first real step to learning anything is to learn *how* to learn. Educators have said the prime rule for learning is to learn something the correct way the first time. If you don't, you are then faced with triple the work. You've learned it. Then you must unlearn it. And then you must relearn the correct information. Doing it this way is a tremendous waste of time.

There are several so-called techniques for learning that will come in handy. For example, remember your first session with a lengthy poem in grade school? In my fifth grade it was Longfellow's poem "Barbara Fritchie." Believe it or not, I can still recite about half of the stanzas of that poem. I learned it by memorization and repetition. Memorization has its place in learning for adults, too, but remember that repetition can result in forgetting if the repetition becomes deadly dull.

One way to absorb information more easily is to understand what you are trying to learn. Information that is understood is retained much longer than knowledge that is merely memorized. Don't consider anything really learned until you fully understand it and can use it in its proper context in your work, or social life.

Similarly, practice in a routine task can make it appear that a person is highly skilled in his job. Too often a man with 20 years on his job has just relearned it for the twentieth time over. He will probably never take the effort to try to improve his work.

Where Can You Learn?

The best way to improve and to increase your knowledge is to analyze what methods you need to reach your goals. Then make every effort to acquire these skills. In some industries, associations run technical, sales, and management training programs. In addition, the American Management Association, the American Marketing Association, the Sales Executive Clubs, and many other national groups provide courses that cut across industry lines.

The federal government, through such organizations as the Small Business Administration, and the various state governments, also provide a variety of courses. Locally, many high schools have adult education classes that may provide the skills you require. Many universities, colleges, and specialty schools provide both seminars and extension courses for adults. You can go for a degree, or attend one or two nights a week just for self-improvement.

This tremendous variety of courses will provide you with a wide range of information. You can learn about the latest techniques needed for your own job, or you can learn how to speed up your reading, improve your writing, step up your learning efficiency, or develop your memory. Later chapters in this book will provide you with background information and techniques for improving your ability in some of these personal areas.

Treasure House at Your Fingertips

Books can be real treasure houses of knowledge for you in your efforts to gain knowledge. Currently, many hardcover and paperback editions are available to the businessperson-student. You might say these are your personal consultants. For a very little investment, you can put the knowledge of the experts at your fingertips. None but the very largest business organizations can afford to hire all the consultants they need. You can acquire the knowledge of any expert for the simple price of a book.

Many publishers now make available a wide variety of self-improvement, management, sales, and technical books that will help both the experienced businessperson and those on the way up.

Motivating Yourself

Another secret of learning is to be highly motivated—to want deeply to acquire certain knowledge. You may feel it would be nice to be president of your company or to be the owner of the biggest independent business in town. But there is a difference between thinking how nice it would be and actually being motivated to reach your goal.

More than likely, most of us tend to remember a fact or bit of information only as long as we think it necessary to do so. One college professor gave a group of businesspeople attending a seminar certain information. He divided his class into three groups. One section was told it would need the information for three days; another for a week. The third group understood they would need the information indefinitely. Follow-up testing showed that in 95 percent of the cases the people retained the information only as long as they were told they would need it. They then promptly forgot it.

This case does show that once motivation is removed, a person tends to forget what he's learned. From a practical standpoint, then, the businessperson-student should do a thorough job of selling himself or herself on the rewards that will come from learning and retaining knowledge. If the desire for these rewards is strong enough, you can gain the necessary motivation to learn what is necessary for your advancement.

Getting More out of Reading

If your learning requires that you do a great deal of reading, here are some tips to help you absorb what you have read:

1. **Relate what you read to your own experiences.**
   Slower, more accurate learning is often faster than a speedy effort. You would be wise to think of specific examples that will relate to your studies as you read, rather than just rush to complete each chapter.
2. **Take a break when you feel the need for one.**
   This often gives the information time to sink in.
3. **Provide yourself with periods of relaxation after attempting some very "heavy" learning.**
   The more complete your relaxation the better, since upsets may cause you to fail to retain your newfound knowledge.
4. **Stop studying when you get tired.**
   Learning slows down when fatigue steps in.
5. **Use every possible aid to help you absorb information.**
   If possible turn off the phone. If you are working at a desk, see that it is neither too low nor too high so that your body must assume an uncomfortable position. Don't use a chair that is too soft, because learning is something we usually consider a chore, and we may begin to doze off if the chair is too comfortable. Have a good reading light properly placed over your shoulder or over the desk and focused right on the paper. Remember, too, that a temperature of 67–70 degrees with humidity at 50 percent is best for you to stay alert.

Your pencil or pen can also be a very valuable study aid. As you read, underline what you think important. Underlining offers you two major rewards. First, you are compelled to stay mentally alert so that you are more apt to find the important. Second, underlining helps you review. The underlined high spots are quickly spotted and redigested.

The best ways to use your pencil or pen for underlining are:

1. Underline topic sentences, key words, and phrases as you read.
2. If you find a series of sentences or paragraphs you want to remember, draw a vertical line to the right or left of this material.
3. If questions or thoughts are raised in your mind by the text, note them in the margins. These notations will serve as a reminder or memory-jogger when you reread the material.

Brief It Down

One of my friends, a lawyer, has a technique which I've found extremely valuable for assimilating information. His legal firm assigned him to patent law work, and he was asked to return to school for one year to pick up some engineering background. He found his return to the books difficult until he remembered his legal training. He began to write briefs for each lesson. These were actually summaries that proved to be his key study tool before an exam. He'd try to limit each brief of a chapter to about one or two hundred words. This mental exercise helped him better understand what he had read.

A businesspaper editor friend prides himself on reading a piece and then briefing it down to a lead paragraph, as if each article was a news story for his readers. What he was actually doing was *practicing* by pretending he was teaching his readers what he, himself, had learned.

Retaining What You Have Learned

We've already mentioned the importance of motivating yourself to retain what you have learned. There are other things that will help you keep this hard-earned information. Once you've learned something, use it as soon and as often as possible, because practice does help you become more perfect. And try to use accurately what you've learned.

Try also to relate your new knowledge to your existing store of information. Not only will you bolster your past experience with new facts, but making continued use of new knowledge sets it more firmly in your mind. Another tip: you should begin to build source files about your job and interests. Clip magazine and newspaper articles. Either purchase books about your field or develop a bibliography of titles for quick reference. This collection of facts can be one of your most valued possessions.

With these guidelines, you have the basis for continuing to absorb new knowledge in an effective manner for as long as you live. As you use this information in your everyday work, you will find that your knowledge, like fine silver, will improve with use.

5
How to Be Boss of Your Desk Work

A man or woman reaching for success is like a rocket aimed into outer space. The rocket has to free itself of the pull of gravity. You or I have to escape from the clutches of the paperwork that ties us to our desks.

I've met people who've felt that keeping their desks piled high with work made them look important. In most cases, their associates and superiors were really not impressed—they felt the overcrowded desk was really a sign of disorganization.

Unfortunately, paperwork and details are a major part of today's business life. The only way you can beat this affliction is to find ways to reduce your desk work.

How to Be Inefficient

A first step is to admit that you are not quite as effective in your work as you thought you were. The major culprits are those who:

1. Tend to make useless and extra work out of every job they face.
2. Insist on doing all the detail work that really could be passed on to an assistant or someone who is qualified to handle the task. Remember, one of management's first rules is that the lowest-paid qualified person should do the work.

3. Allow work to pile up to such a degree that they are unable to handle real emergencies when they occur.

4. Refuse to make decisions when they first need making. They keep shunting the papers from one pile to another, and every time they show up at the top of a pile, they waste more time refreshing their memories with the pertinent facts.

Organization Will End the Log Jam

You can conquer these weaknesses. You've already learned that you must be boss. You must manage yourself. Beating the busy desk bugaboo simply means learning how to organize your work, your day, and your desk.

The person who develops techniques for handling incoming and outgoing paperwork will stay on top of the job. In recent years I've discussed the problem of the "paper flood" with executives from many different types of businesses. They had many suggestions for speeding paperwork. On the pages that follow in this chapter, I've gathered the best of these ideas to help you stay on top of your work.

Most important: Try to avoid as much work as possible. While it may sound odd for an executive to avoid work, it's really not, if you are simply dividing and managing your work according to a plan.

How do you divide up your work among others? Let your secretary handle details for you. Next, put your assistant to work handling all possible remaining tasks. Then take a good look at what is left for you and see if there is any more work you can shift to either your secretary or your assistant.

Let's take a moment to look at this matter of an assistant. Perhaps you don't rate one today. You will tomorrow. It's a wise step to develop a good assistant. Besides taking a big load off your shoulders, it can give you a real feeling of security. When it is time for a vacation or a business trip, you'll be able to go knowing that you've left a person ready and able to take over for you. Then again, if promotion comes for you, you've trained someone to step into your place. In many companies, the measure of a manager is the ability to develop others.

Stay Out of Their Hair

Once you've trained your assistant and your secretary to help you, quit trying to keep your "fingers in every pie." You build confidence in your people only by giving them a chance to act on their own. Once you've assigned work, it should only be brought to your attention if something seems amiss.

If your people do run into a problem, see that they bring suggestions along to a problem conference. In this way, you need only make a decision based on the facts they present. The added advantage here is that your people learn to think for themselves.

It's another good rule of management to not meddle with those jobs you've given to others. As we said before, the lowest-paid qualified man or woman should be assigned each job.

One further suggestion about your relations with your assistants. Get out of the habit of calling too many conferences. In most cases, all these meetings do is take your people and you away from your work. Too many meetings may also tend to keep your people from making decisions on their own. They'll just sit and wait to hear your opinion, then echo it.

One of my former bosses, a vice president of a major oil company, limited his staff meetings to one a month. He saw to it that every member of his department, from the office boy up to himself and including the secretaries, took turns running the meetings. Not only did they learn responsibility, they also learned to think on their feet. I could also see the interest of these people flame brightly in their work, because they felt they had helped develop the projects.

Letting Your Secretary Help You

Now let's take a few moments to consider your secretary. You hired one to help you, so why not let it happen? Experts estimate that some bosses waste almost half the working time of a secretary by not giving enough responsibility.

One of the first things to do is to let this individual handle your appointment schedule. The secretary should know who you will see and how much time to allow for each visitor, as well as those people you want to talk to over the phone. Then the secretary can use judgment on your other callers.

Another time-consuming job for your secretary to assume is the handling of your files. Don't waste your time looking for papers. Let your secretary file everything and get the papers you need when you need them. Keep out of the files. And don't keep papers on your desk—file them. Otherwise, they have a peculiar penchant for disappearing just when you want them.

When the mail comes to your desk, an experienced secretary should have already separated it into two or three piles. For example, pile one would hold those papers which demand your immediate attention. Pile two would contain those letters which can be answered by your secretary after you've penciled a brief notation on the bottom of each letter. Pile three contains the mail which does not require your immediate action.

Plan your dictation for one regular time each day, either in the morning or the afternoon. In this way, your secretary can plan a schedule to coincide with your demands for time. This regular schedule also allows the secretary to make the best use of time. Most managers told me they preferred to dictate to their secretaries in the morning, right after looking over the mail. This permitted their secretaries to transcribe the dictation and to ask any questions they may have for their bosses before the working day ends. The secretary was then ready to start the next working day fresh, with a clean desk.

These executives also felt firmly that dictation should be limited to once a day, except for emergencies. Irregular dictation schedules waste a secretary's time, they felt. If you share a secretary with one or two others, arranging your schedule for once-a-day dictation is a great help to all concerned.

Another suggestion for helping the secretary in work is to set aside a few minutes each day for you to talk over projects together. This keeps the secretary informed about your current business activities, and also prevents you from being interrupted with questions throughout the day.

Giving the Secretary the Proper Tools

Give your secretary the tools to do the job quickly, accurately, and easily. A good electric typewriter can shorten typing time and also be less tiring. A comfortable chair and desk will also help improve her efficiency.

There is a great variety of dictating equipment available. Such equipment has the advantage of permitting you to dictate whenever and wherever you wish. This is especially true with the small portable units now available. You can dictate at home, in the car, in your office, or anywhere and just turn the record, tape, belt, or cylinder over to your secretary or the typing pool.

A More Efficient You

Now let's get back to the work pile you've left for yourself. First of all, learn how to read faster. We'll devote our next chapter to that, but now let's get down to the specifics of self-management to help you control your desk work.

Earlier we talked about the importance of managing yourself. This ability is never in greater demand than when you must handle miscellaneous desk work. I've put together some rules for managing detail that I have picked up in my travels. Really, they are very simple.

Analyze every job that comes to you and schedule it for a definite time. Too many men and women run around, working at a lot of different jobs at one time and completing none. When you start on a task, finish it. Don't put off making a decision about it. This only means that you must review the whole problem later and still come up with a solution. It's double or triple work for you.

Many people handle the many easy, short-time projects first. They say this helps them warm up. They can then complete the fewer but larger jobs without having the threat of many small tasks hanging over them.

For the big jobs, the best way is to start on the unpleasant ones first, while you are feeling fresh. However, if one project becomes too tough, put it aside for the time being. You can return to it when you are fresher. You'll find that after taking a break you may return to the task with a fresh approach.

One of the best rules is to keep work right in front of you, to haunt you. I think this is the actual philosophy behind these fancy modern desks of ours. In the old roll-top affairs, work was easily pigeonholed out of sight. In contrast, the modern desk is only a work space sitting on either legs or a filing cabinet. Leave the work right on top of the desk. Most of us are orderly enough to be a bit ashamed of others seeing our messy desk. If the work sits out in plain sight, we'll try our best to complete the project.

Look for the Short Cuts

Use whatever short cuts you can find. One of my friends simply returns any letters that do not require filing with his answer written across the bottom. If the letter must be retained, his secretary prepares a letter based on his notations for his signature.

Another handy time-saver is the telephone. You can use it for any matter that does not require documentation. This method is certainly much faster than the mails.

Keep in constant touch with those people who work with you. Such communication will prevent misunderstandings and avoid lost time.

Another suggestion: Keep your door shut. Most executives have learned that it does not pay to keep their office doors wide open to everybody. Too many well-meaning callers are actually time-wasters. You can kill valuable hours every day just talking about sports, fishing, or exchanging the latest jokes. Perhaps you'll be called antisocial, but if you are the least bit capable in your normal relations with your associates, you'll quickly kill this reputation. The quality and quantity of your work will show that you are a man to be counted upon.

As you grow in stature and responsibility, you'll find more and more requests come to you from outside your own business. You'll be asked to serve on committees, to make speeches, to join business and civic groups. This is a sign of recognition. Each of these activities, however, requires some of your valuable time and energy.

Some community or business association work is necessary as your contribution to a stronger local and national community and to the growth of your own industry. It is a good rule, however, to be very selective before you accept any invitation. Pick and choose those activities which can accomplish the most for your own family, or community, or industry, as well as your business.

And as one last suggestion: Watch the briefcase. Too many people get in the habit of carrying their case back and forth to work every night. After a while they lose interest in a constant chain of night work and just go through the motions of packing the case every evening.

If you must take work home, try to do so on just a few nights each week. Each of us must develop a full, well-rounded way of life. This will bring with it peace of mind, greater health, and the vigor to work at keeping your desk cleared and yourself ready for important action.

6
Read Faster to Read Better

Take a close look at your watch as you begin to read the following instructions about the Federal income tax:

If income tax filing is complicated, confusing and time consuming, January 1 is the day to set a simple plan in action. It won't help with your current return, but when preparation time rolls around next year, the job will be a lot simpler and may even save you money by insuring that each and every legal deduction is taken.

A taxpayer's first New Year's resolution should be self-organization. The key is to file away each tax-related item when it's received. By keeping all documents in a single, safe place, they will be ready when the time comes to prepare next year's forms. The taxpayer will avoid the mad scramble to gather misplaced receipts and other documents in time for the April 15 federal filing deadline.

Taxpayers should save medical, dental and drug receipts, proof of interest charges, state and local tax documents, charitable receipts and notes on undocumented cash contributions. An adequate retention system should hold the year's bills, invoices, receipts and cancelled checks.

At filing time, the individual can then present his or her tax preparation service with an orderly, complete package of materials with which to work; or personally approach the job without having to constantly stop and search for missing items.

Records to be kept include any documents reflecting income. Wages are normally reported on a W-2 form supplied by employers. However, records should be kept on all interest and dividend income, profits or losses from sales of property and securities, and all other money received. A good rule of thumb is to file everything that relates to receiving or spending money. It's much easier to discard an unneeded document than to search for a receipt or statement that's been misplaced or even discarded.

Here are several additional suggestions for taxpayers:

1. Pay all tax-deductible items by check. Reviewing your checkbook provides an immediate picture of your deductions. It's wise to retain the bills, sales slips and any receipts for these checks should a deduction have to be proven. This is especially true for medical expenses which may have been reimbursed in part by insurance coverages.

2. Retain past income tax forms for at least six years. They are helpful if you have a "windfall" and wish to average income over a five-year period.

3. Keep a log or diary of expenses incurred while doing charitable work, including information such as the number of miles driven, and the amounts spent for meals, parking and tolls. Credit cards purchases of gas are not considered proof of travel.

4. File records of long-term expenses such as home improvements and investments. These are needed to verify profit and loss when a home or other investment is finally sold.

5. Take a close look at your own state tax laws. They may allow deductions not permitted by the federal government.

The entire question of income taxes often is complicated, regardless of the amounts of money involved. We recommend that expert counsel be obtained when any doubt or question exists about income tax matters.

You've just read some 520 words. This is the type of reading the business men and women must do, all the time. If you have what is considered good speed-reading ability, it should have taken you just about three-quarters of a minute to read this excerpt. If you failed to come closer than three minutes, you are probably lost in a paperwork jungle.

This might sound a bit extreme, but it is true. One look at your everyday mail and the intracompany correspondence which pours over your desk will point out this job requirement. You must be able to read fast if you are to do the required work.

Reading, Just Reading

At a meeting of the American Management Association some time ago, conferees said that executives spent between 25 and 75 percent of their time just reading. This work load consisted of reading memos and reports, general correspondence, business and trade publications, product bulletins, advertising materials, and other assorted printed matter.

It was also reported that employees at other levels spent up to two hours of every day reading.

Since the average reader crawls along reading about 200 to 250 words per minute, it stands to reason that the best investment you can make is to improve your reading ability. Say you can boost it from this low mark of 250 words per minute up to 500. You'll have cut your reading time in half. If you can raise it to about 700 (the figure the experts consider necessary for an adult) you might be able to read everything you need to in only 40 percent of the time you now spend. Since every minute you save is worth money to your career, it really pays to learn how you can convert reading time to dollars.

Read as an Adult

We actually have only two major defenses against the paper flood. We can throw as much as possible into the waste-basket, or we can learn to read as an adult should.

Yes, I said as an adult! Too many of us have a set of reading skills that are stagnated at the level of a sixth-grade student. It's not really our fault. We were taught to read by methods that are inadequate to meet the demands of the modern business world.

Like many skills that we fail to develop to the fullest, we stopped learning to read at a young age. Some of us actually begin to regress, and our reading ability is simply an understanding of the meaning of the common words and the habit of reading from left to right.

Luckily, reading skills can be improved at any age. You can advance from a mediocre 250 words per minute to 700 or even 1,000 or more words per minute. With this greater ability will come improved understanding and self-growth.

Slowpokes Don't Really Understand More

One of the great fallacies is the belief that a slow reader understands and remembers more. It's just not so. Reading specialists have found that the faster you can move down a page, the more you will have the opportunity to comprehend. This has been proven time and time again by tests of college students. They prove that a good reader picks out the essential ideas and puts together the "big picture."

Like most rules, there is an exception. We must understand that certain types of material naturally slow us down. This often may be the result of our own interest level, and why most of us will race through fiction and seemingly crawl through a company report.

Your Mind—The Key
to Good Reading Habits

The basic idea in the modern reading schools is that your mind controls the act of reading. A slow reader may make ten or even twenty eye movements for each printed line. A faster reader will comprehend the same line in only two or three eye movements. The secret, therefore, is to make your mind read efficiently.

The good reader attacks a printed page as if he or she were eating in a restaurant. The menu, instructions to the waiter, and the arrival of the food tell how to go about the act of eating. In like manner, the good reader quickly checks the title, chapter, subheadings, picture captions if there are any, and the first paragraph to see if he or she must read the piece at all.

This investigation also tells how fast you'll have to read and how much you can expect to get out of the material.

Like the diner eating you must also have a strong sense of purpose before reading anything. You must know what you are reading, why you are reading it, and how much you will profit by reading it.

How to Pick Up Speed

Let's list some rules or guides for faster reading. These will be expanded later in this chapter.

1. **Preview your material.**
   Check titles, subheads, captions, and first paragraphs to determine if the material is worth reading and what reading speed is required.
2. **Don't look back.**
   Once you've started, keep moving on. Avoid the temptation to go back and look again at some of the ideas you may feel you don't fully understand. You can come back to review later, after the entire piece is finished.
3. **Find the main ideas.**
   Discover the one idea in each paragraph that is important. Also note the directional signals such as: "also," "such as," "but," "yet," "etc."
4. **Memorize.**
   As you read, select the facts that are important to you. Store them away in your brain and memorize them for future use.

Now, let's put these rules to work at helping us to read faster and to get more out of what we are reading.

Reading by Thought Units

You can gain speed by simply reading in longer thought units. This is a matter of recognizing entire groups of words instead of picking up each word one at a time. This is more easily done than it would seem, because the writers put sentences together with key words and phrases. The other words and phrases are actually just subsidiaries to the main thought.

If you will follow the key words, moving your eyes from one sense group to the next, you will soon find yourself pausing only two or three times a line. The slower reader is constantly running into road blocks and detours hopping from one word to the next, making 10 or 20 or more hops before they finish a line.

Earlier we said good readers analyze what they read before actually starting. They are usually flexible and able to slip from one speed to another, based on the requirements of the material after previewing it. The good reader also quickly makes the decision to try to master all the facts or to merely look for essential ideas.

Working with the Author

Once the preview is complete, you dive in and begin communicating with the author. Don't fight the writers. If they are the least bit good, they have placed the idea on a word pedestal so that you can quickly find it. This is usually true because the well-written sentence contains only one important idea.

Your reading will speed up as you learn to ignore such things as transitions, connections, and modifiers. When you've done this, all you have left are the main subject and verb. Then you isolate the main idea and subsidiary thoughts. You have a clear understanding of what the writer meant, and you can move right on to the next paragraph.

Your reading movement is assisted by the so-called "directional words" that move you along from one important idea to the next. These are words the author has put there to help you. Your mind should only glance at them, and move right on to isolate the major thought. The directional words are then forgotten.

Such directional words include: "and," "also," "likewise," "such as," "furthermore," "in addition to." These words simply tell you that the author will introduce no new ideas or changes in thought. The track ahead is cleared for you to read on at top speed.

There are other connecting words, however, which are designed to flag your attention. They tell you to look out for a change. These words include: "but," "yet," "otherwise," "although," and "on the other hand."

Mining the Gold

The skilled reader is like a locomotive. Keeping on a straight track, he or she is not interested in the words themselves, only in what the writer is trying to say. Again it is a matter of seeking out the main points and ideas of the author. You don't let the details bog you down. When you've finished each piece, you understand just what the author meant, even if you don't remember the exact words he used to get his idea across.

Remembering details and facts requires that you pick out what you want to retain. You then organize these prized facts and store them away in a corner of your brain for future use.

Skimming for Greater Speed

Many of the fastest readers have the ability to skim. They use a wide glance of their eyes to preview upcoming facts. These skimmers recognize key words and ideas. They have trained themselves to understand a writer's attempts at organization.

Skimmers of the slow variety read by the lines. Their faster compatriots draw a mental line down the center of the page. They read only the words on either side of the line, and miss very little of importance.

What actually happens is two things. First, the skimmer's eyes are picking up and interpreting the words alongside the words they actually read through what is called peripheral vision. Peripheral vision is the reason for the success of many athletes and good drivers. You can practice to achieve such a wide glance.

Second, a good reader has a sense of organization. Knowledge of the language and subject is such that this person is able to infer the total meaning from the facts the author has placed on either side of the invisible line. Skimming is a most valuable technique, but it takes long practice to master this art.

Practice Makes Perfect

Once you are able to read more, you will find that you are able as well to keep up with the latest ideas in your field. This ability can mean a promotion if you work for others. If you have your own business, it can mean increased prosperity because you've learned new ideas and techniques.

Once you have reached what you consider good reading speed, keep the ability at peak performance. You can do this only by regular and constant practice. No matter what you pick up to read, peruse it at your top speed for facts and ideas. The literature can be fiction, light nonfiction, a technical report, or a memo from the boss.

We've spent this chapter describing how a person can increase speed and understanding through faster, more accurate reading. If you want, you can do it yourself by constantly trying to step up your speed. In addition, there are speed reading courses available from specialized speed reading schools and through many of the nation's colleges.

Many men and women have practiced by simply setting an alarm clock and then timing themselves to see how many words they read. They continually try to improve on their past performance. Others do it a bit more scientifically— they tally up the seconds it takes them to complete an article, chapter, or report, divide this figure into the total number of words, then multiply by 60 to convert their total words per minute.

No matter what method you use to step up your reading speed, the payoff can mean more efficiency. With this efficiency will come greater success for you.

7
Stay Healthy to Accomplish More

To manage your own business or to do the job for another person at the fullest efficiency, your body must be able to meet all demands forced upon it. If you are tired all the time, if you find it difficult to meet constant pressures, you are operating under a severe handicap. It could destroy your business or your career.

To be physically fit is to be in good health. Unfortunately, we seldom think of the state of our health until illness strikes. Then it is often too late to do anything about it. You know your business or job inside and out. You keep up with the latest techniques and tools. You look for short cuts. Why else would you be reading this book? Yet, how many of you have ever taken the trouble to find out how to keep the marvelous machine we call the body working at full strength?

A few health hints kept in mind while you are well will help *keep* you fit. Here are a few suggestions for you.

Proper Fuel Is Required

The fuel for our body is the food we eat. Americans pride themselves on an abundance of nourishing and tastily prepared foods of endless variety. And rightly we should. Today, children grow taller, stronger, and healthier than their ancestors did, largely because of better and more plentiful food, rich in minerals and vitamins.

With all these advantages on our side, many of us, through poor habits, eat improperly. Some of us eat foods high in caloric value and low in vitamins and other essential food nutrients. These are so-called "empty" calories. If their intake is continued over a long period of time, they often result in an overweight person with a relatively poor resistance to illness.

Others eat excessive amounts of fat, especially those of the saturated type found in meat, butter, and cheese. A diet that is excessively high in such fats may predispose a person to early arteriosclerosis and coronary heart disease.

The food you eat provides not only fuel for warmth and energy, it also regulates many of your bodily functions. Improper diet may reduce your resistance to disease, may impair vision, and may cause skin disturbances and other kinds of ailments.

What Is a Good Diet?

What is a good diet? It is one that is moderate in calories, balanced in the proportions of various food substances, rich in vitamins and minerals, and relatively low in fats, especially those of the saturated variety.

It is wise to remember a few rules about the makeup of the food that fuels our body.

Proteins are said to be the building blocks of the body. They help our bodies repair damaged tissues, develop muscles, and provide other necessary body fluids. Proteins are found in meat, fish, fowl, and cheese.

Carbohydrates supply the quick energy we need. They are found in sugars and starches. Fats are also required to give us energy and to develop the heat our body requires.

A good diet implies that food will be eaten regularly at regular times. Your diet should be varied and diversified. You should allow yourself sufficient time for a leisurely meal. This is most important in combating the buildup of tensions, as we will see in Chapter 7. Overeating should be avoided.

Some of us will, by choice, select a diet of good variety. However, if you find yourself overweight or underweight, or just not feeling up to par, it would be wise to consult your physician and include in the discussion a study of your dietary habits.

Exercise Is Important

A certain amount of exercise is required if you are to stay physically fit. It is not necessary for you to go into heavy training as an athlete would, but a proper amount of exercise compatible with your age and body is of definite benefit.

Aside from keeping your muscles and body in shape, exercise will help relax mental tensions and ease a tired mind. A feeling of well-being that follows a period of exercise will help you over the periods of lassitude and fatigue that frequently follow a trying day's work.

Your exercise should be regularly scheduled and it should be geared to your own physical characteristics. Here, your physician should be consulted to suggest the best exercises for you. For those in the older age groups, simple calisthenics or sitting-up exercises are adequate and beneficial. For the more agile, swimming, handball, tennis, or golf may be more appropriate.

Luckily, you can exercise frequently and without too much preparation. For example:

1. **Walk whenever and wherever you can.**
   If you must take a bus to the office, get off six or eight blocks early. The tempo of your walking will awaken your mind and set you up, ready for work. Take a walk after lunch. Some experts recommend that we spend at least one hour walking every day.

2. **Work around your home.**

    Push the lawn mower and other garden tools with vigor. When you have to move a chair, pick it up and carry it—don't just push it.

3. **Climb stairs every day.**

    It gives your knees a chance to bend and your legs a chance to lift your body.

4. **Use every possible opportunity to exercise.**

    Don't sit down to put on your shoes. Stand up and reach over to get them on. This kind of bending every morning will help you stay in shape. When you bathe, stoop and bend your body as you wash and dry yourself.

Adequate Rest Is Essential

As equally important as exercise is proper rest. Sleep is vital in helping you recover from mental and physical fatigue. Without sufficient sleep, you can quickly become irritable, restless, and inefficient.

Many of us fail to get enough sleep simply because we can't afford to spend the full eight hours necessary each night. Others may be unable to sleep enough for a variety of reasons; such insomnia may be due to physical illness, emotional strain, worry, or excessive amounts of coffee or other stimulants.

You can help yourself to more relaxed sleep by setting up conditions that are conducive to good sleeping. See that the room temperature and humidity are comfortable. Choose a mattress that is just right for your back. If you have eaten heavily, walk around the block before you climb into bed.

Try to forget your business or your job or other worries. One way to do this is to relax in bed with an interesting book. Another way is to take a relaxing shower or a warm bath.

Some of us worry so much about not being able to fall asleep that we get tense and just can't sleep. Try to stop worrying about falling asleep. Once your head hits the pillow, just relax. Sleep will come.

If you are troubled with insomnia, act fast to find out what is wrong because it can undermine your health. If you cannot correct the insomnia by simple means, your physician should be consulted promptly.

Your Eyes and Ears

Of our five senses, sight and hearing are probably the most important. Safeguarding them should be foremost in your mind in considering your physical fitness.

The eye is made up of many kinds of specialized tissues controlled by muscles and nerves. It is protected by a layer of cushioning fat set in a bony framework which protects all but the exposed portion. Your eye is a miniature camera, complete with lens and the iris as the diaphragm.

Although your eyes are placed in a position that provides them with a good deal of protection, they are still subject to many types of injury. These include damage by dust, fumes, chemicals, and excessive ultraviolet radiation which may be encountered in sunlight or from a welder's arc. If you should be exposed to such hazards, it is important to remember to wear protective glasses or goggles. Many types have been designed to meet the different occupational dangers.

Aside from injuries, your eyes are subject to a number of ills. Many persons are born with eyes with lenses which have slight defects in their contour or shape. To enable their eyes to function properly, it is necessary to correct the defect with glasses. Children who do poorly in school are often those who are handicapped by faulty vision and require eyeglasses.

Current living and business practice demands more and more use of your eyes, and it is very important to have them checked periodically. Television has added another heavy burden to our already overworked eyes.

In later years, the eyes may be subject to such diseases as glaucoma and cataracts. If they are detected early, much can be done to delay the progress of these disabling infirmities. A competent ophthalmologist with special equipment can quickly ascertain whether or not signs of these diseases are developing.

Take Care of Your Hearing

Some people feel that hearing is even more important than sight. Hearing failures often manifest themselves in the middle years of life. They can be caused by a variety of things. Some hearing problems come simply from an accumulation of wax in the ear canals. This accumulation can be easily removed by a physician. Other hearing problems are caused by the scarring and immobilization of the tiny bones which conduct sounds in the middle ear. Such deafness can often be helped by surgery.

Other types of deafness are caused by degeneration of the nerves which conduct the sound impulses from the ear to the brain. Such types of deafness can be helped by having fitted a proper type of hearing aid.

Infections are frequent in the ears. Earaches or running ears should send you promptly to a physician for treatment so any permanent ear damage may be avoided. You should report any signs of diminishing hearing to your physician. Then the physician can determine the cause and begin proper treatment without delay.

Don't Forget Those Physical Checkups

The importance of periodic checkups by your physician cannot be overstressed. Most of us consult a doctor only if we are seriously ill or have have some serious injury or accident. Some of us take the trouble to see our physician for more minor ills. Very few of us actually see our physician for a general physical examination every year.

Periodic examinations have many important advantages. Aside from discovering illnesses or diseases in their early stages when they are more amenable to treatment, annual examinations permit your physician to know you and your body when you are well. Thus you will be treated more effectively when you are ill. Your doctor can guide you and help you to stay well.

You will find that medical checkups vary in scope, but they usually include the following procedures:

1. A general examination which includes listening to your heart and lungs with a stethoscope.

> Most abnormalities in these two organs can be discovered by a thorough general physical examination.

2. A chest X-ray is important to discover if you have such diseases of the lungs as tuberculosis, and to indicate whether the outline of the heart and large blood vessels is normal.

3. A blood pressure determination is a simple, painless measurement, performed by wrapping an inflatable bag, connected to a meter, around your arm.

> From the blood pressure measurement, your physician will gain important information as to the state of your circulation and general health.

4. A urinalysis is of great value in detecting diseases of the kidneys, as well as other unrelated diseases such as diabetes.

Putting together the results of the examination, laboratory tests, and such information as you bring regarding the way you feel, your doctor gains a good picture of the state of your health.

He may make some recommendations, such as taking off excess weight. He may prescribe some treatment for a disorder that he has discovered. Or everything may be in good order. If the latter is the case, you'll have reason to leave the office with the feeling of elation and well-being that comes from the knowledge that you are physically fit and capable of meeting every test thrown at you.

8
Taking the Tension Out of Your Job

Are you spending 10, 12, or 14 hours a day on your job? Chances are that some of this time is wasted, and that this waste is brought on by tension. Luckily, there are ways to overcome the mental or nervous strains that cause tension to build up.

First of all, let's see where these tensions and pressures come from. Tension is not a new disease which affects us when we become adults. Most of us have lived with these pressures since birth. At first, there were the unconscious pressures to learn to walk and talk. As we grew older, we met the pressures of tests in school, of making the team or club, of getting a date or getting married, or finding a job or starting your own business.

Today, we face almost constant pressures. Most of us go through mental changes when we are stimulated by a problem or irritation of some sort. Tension can arise both on the job and in our social lives. Tension can develop because we are rushing to complete a job within a definite span of time. It may arise if we need to meet a dollar or item quota in selling, or to face a load of bills, or even if we need money to get married or to send our children to college. As we are given added responsibility over work and people, we also receive new pressures.

Part of the battle is simply to understand that your work will bring about tension, and that these pressures often will be the real cause of both a tired feeling and poor job or social performance.

The Animals Have It Easy

Our big problem is that a natural release from tension does not come easy. An irritated animal may strike out at its tormentors. What happens if a customer calls to "give you hell" for something that is not your fault? Or suppose the boss forgets a promised bonus? Right away you become angry—and you tense up. You'd like to punch your boss or the customer in the nose, but that is impossible. In fact, you can't let either know how irritated you are.

So you begin to steam under the collar. Soon the tension has backed up and you've got a headache, or a backache, or maybe an upset stomach. You feel awful. Your work, what there is of it that you *do* finish, suffers. The rest piles up so that you start tomorrow with a load of today's work facing you.

How to Avoid Tension Buildup

You can avoid all such tension and keep operating at top efficiency—if you act to keep tension from building up in the first place.

We know of two ways to overcome tension. The first is exercise, that activity that too many of us either forget or ignore. But exercise is not the full answer. Where it fails to provide complete relief, a program of self-management will often provide the solution.

Just where does tension seem to build up in you? For most of us the uncomfortableness seems to stay localized in our neck or shoulder muscles or down our back. Tension can be dispelled from these areas by a series of physical actions you can take to stop the buildup. A training director for a large coporation, speaking at a convention I attended some years ago, suggested the following exercises to men and women chained to their desks in a sedentary job. Here they are:

1. Stretch your arms and take a deep breath every time you sit down.
2. Every 10 or 15 minutes, straighten up and then shrug your shoulders to relax yourself.
3. Lean back in your chair and have a good stretch every half-hour.
4. Don't keep your phone at your elbow. Set it so that you have to stretch to reach it and put it back.
5. Lean over and touch your toes every time you get ready to stand up.

These are five very simple exercises. Practice them until they become second nature to you. You'll be surprised how well they help you to keep tension at bay.

Try Desk "P.T."

It would be wonderful if everyone of us could or would spend an hour every day exercising. Unfortunately, very few of us can find the time to do so. Even if we could, how many actually would?

Suppose you could shut the door of your office, or draw an invisible screen around you if you work in a "bull pen." The first thing you should do would be a few quick push-ups. Then you'd touch your toes five or 10 times. If you did this, you would have toned yourself up for the whole day in just about five minutes' time.

The trouble is, who will do it? Some of us would be too embarrassed by what the boss or our co-workers or employees would say. Others of us are just too lazy.

These two exercises were out of the question for a magazine editor I once worked with. However, he resorted to what he called "Desk P.T." One of the best of his exercises is a sort of chair push-up. Try it as a quick tension reliever.

Place one hand on each arm of your chair. Push down until your arms have straightened out and you have raised your body out of the chair. Now, let yourself down and raise yourself up and out of your chair again. Do five or 10 of these two or three times a day.

Another of his office exercises was a so-called desk push-up. In this exercise you lean against your desk, with your hands touching the desk. Now use your hands to push yourself out and away from the desk until you are standing straight. Now back down and then out until you are again standing straight. Do 10 of these at a time. The desk push-up is not strenuous, but it is a good toner-up. It is less work than a prone push-up from the floor, and it really seems to help dispel tension.

Avoid slumping in your chair. This puts an uncomfortable weight on the base of your spine. Assume a posture that will enable you to breathe properly.

The Atmosphere Is Important, Too

Try to avoid working in a stuffy room. If ventilation is poor, you'll have to make a greater effort to complete your work. To function most efficiently, your brain cells must have plenty of fresh air.

Incidentally, you won't tire as quickly if your office or place of work is kept at 67-70 degrees. If the temperature drops lower or climbs higher, your body needs more energy to operate at fullest efficiency. Tests have shown that at 90 degrees your body expends 50 percent more energy than if the temperature is at 67–70 degrees.

Rest periods are as vital to a mental laborer as to a physical laborer. The type of relaxation required, however, can be completely different. The physical laborer needs complete relaxation. In contrast, the mental laborer should engage in a mildly stimulating activity to keep alertness at the proper level. You might play cards or chess, or read a book or a newspaper.

Exercising Away from the Office

You should follow some sort of regular physical condition- ing to keep your body toned up and the tension down. In our last chapter we discussed exercise and walking. Both are vitally important as aids in keeping your performance tip- top.

Actually, you can do much to keep yourself fit while you are commuting to your place of business. Use the stairs as much as possible. Walk to and from train or parking lot. At lunchtime, take a walk. One of the best ways to digest your food is to take a walk to admire the sights. More often than not, you'll come back with your mind cleared and ready for an afternoon's business.

Let me advance another radical thought. Take your whole family for an after-dinner walk. You will all feel better for it and sleep will come that much faster than if you all had slumped down in front of your television set.

I have my own formula for relaxing at night, even when I have to break a rule and bring some important work home. As soon as I finish kissing the family, I take the dog for a walk— just short of a half-mile each way. Then I wash up and change clothes, and we all sit down for supper.

After supper, I relax with the kids. Then I do anything that needs doing—a do-it-yourself project that my wife has thought up, the rare office work, attend a civic meeting, or just plain relaxation. Before going to bed, I take the dog for his last walk of the night. Then I shower and I'm off to bed.

Incidentally, scientists at the University of California say the quickest and most effective way to banish physical tired- ness is to climb under a cold shower. Perhaps it is a shock, but it does work.

Ask Your Doctor First

There is no doubt about it, engaging in a regular program of exercise of one kind or another will help you stay in shape and keep tension from developing. The only reason for not exercising is physical. Each person's case depends upon his or her own condition. The best thing to do is to ask your doctor to prescribe the best conditioning program for you.

Self-Management Is Also Important

Now, let's discuss the other method for minimizing job pressures. It is simply the self-management techniques we are discussing in this book. One way to avoid strain and pressure is to have your job under your thumb.

With good self-management, you quickly isolate your problems and find out what causes them. Next, you decide on the best way to solve these problems. The methods for self-management of your time and for cutting deskwork described in Chapters, 1, 2, and 4 will do much to help you to a happier, healthier business life and the resulting satisfactory home life.

9
Getting More Out of Conventions

How many conventions are held annually? Look at the "Today's Activities" boards at hotels and conference and convention centers and you'll find more than 30,000 on the calendar each year. The cost to business is in the billions.

These sessions range all the way from social gatherings, which resemble nothing so much as a family reunion, to highly technical meetings carefully designed to bring their audiences the most advanced and expert information concerning their businesses. The millions of people who attend these conventions not only make convention-going a multibillion dollar-a-year business, but one of the country's favorite pastimes.

After 30 years or so of attending such meetings I'm convinced that the great majority are essentially a three-ring circus of meetings, product showings and hospitality rooms, all vying for attention.

Active Participation

Unlike the circus, where attendance is strictly on a spectator basis, convention going can be a participating as well as a spectator sport. It can be, that is, *if* you have the constitution to permit it. But if the mere thought of standing up before an audience of more than two people gives you butterflies in the stomach, forget about speechmaking and enjoy your convention as a listener.

As a spectator, how do you go about getting back in equivalent value an outlay which may run to several hundred dollars? While the exact amount depends upon how expensive your tastes are, or your budget permits them to be, the investment at today's costs will be a sizable one, and you and your company deserve some return. Whether you get it or not depends to a large extent on how well you plan and how carefully you follow through.

Begin Planning Ahead

Your planning starts with the first notice of the convention details, such as date, location, headquarters hotel and the program you receive. If you are wise (and experienced) you'll get your hotel reservations in EARLY. Send in your request to the convention bureau or reservations manager designated to handle such reservations for your convention.

This will insure that you get a room at the special rates arranged for by the convention committee. It will also insure that you will be "among the in-crowd" and in the middle of things, including the possibility of a snake dance through your room or some golf practice in the corridor. You may even be "lucky" enough to be sandwiched between two hospitality rooms, an ideal spot for one who is lonesome when not in crowds. An early reservation can also permit you to avoid this form of torture, or at least give you a fighting chance to make a change while there still is time.

Looking for Peace and Quiet

If, on the other hand you would like greater peace and quiet, and some seclusion from the crowds, try making your reservation directly with the hotel, specifying not too noticeably that it is in connection with the convention. Your chances of getting a room somewhat removed from a focal point of informal activity and noise are good.

If you want still more seclusion, make your reservations at a hotel other than the headquarters hotel and say nothing about the convention. However, this last advice should be qualified. If you select a hotel too far removed from the site of meetings, you'll find yourself involved in excess travel back and forth. And you will miss much of the good fellowship that is an important part of this rite of American life.

Where to Sleep

In any event, I suggest that when selecting your accommodations, you specify a middle-priced room, unless you are trying to impress your spouse (if he or she is going) or business acquaintances. In fact, you may, with a little luck, end up with a higher-priced room if the hotel management must honor your reservation in the face of a room shortage. On the other hand, don't commit yourself to a bottom-priced room without a prior inspection, unless you can live comfortably in a broom closet.

The same general rule of "get it in early" applies to travel reservations. Select your route or method of travel, then pin down suitable accommodations as soon as you can. And include return reservations. If there is anything less appealing than a standby slot in an airline terminal or railroad station at the end of a convention, I've yet to find it.

Last but not least, get acknowledgment of your reservations from both hotel and mode of travel. Tuck these away where they will be safe, and be sure to carry them with you. You'd be surprised how many slips there can be between your request and the final delivery, and you may have to enforce your rights.

Set Your Targets

As a final step in your advance preparation, make a list of the things you want to accomplish at the convention—the questions you want answered, the products and supplies you want to check on, the people you want to meet, the meetings you want to attend. If your convention committee has been properly considerate, you will receive a program in advance. Use it.

You are now ready for the convention. Register promptly when you arrive. If you were thoughtful enough to register in advance (most convention arrangements now make this possible), you will have saved yourself a little time and trouble at this point. If not, an early visit to the registration desk will get these formalities out of the way in fairly short and comfortable order. Many organizations arrange for advance registrations for their members and guests.

Get Your Bearings

Get your final program, and your bearings. This is the best time to find out exactly where the meeting rooms are, where the exhibits will be located, and where the hospitality rooms are, if you are interested.

If you are lucky, manufacturers and suppliers will be posted on the hotel lobby bulletin board and not too inaccessible from the registration desk. If not, a little judicious inquiry at the desk or of the nearest friendly-looking person who also looks informed, will be necessary. A little trouble at this point will save a lot of extra walking and hunting later on.

Doing the Town

If you want to sightsee or otherwise "do the town," the hotel will be more than pleased to furnish information about local entertainment and other features offered by the host city. Most city hotels have well-documented, pocket sized directories designed to sell you on the local what-to-do. More sedate activities are usually arranged for wives by a committee assigned to provide for the comforts and entertainment of the distaff guests.

At this point it might be wise to supply an off-the-program tip: If you must "do the town," arrange to arrive early enough so that you can perform this chore before the convention begins. For one thing you are less likely to be seen where you wouldn't be caught dead with someone you wouldn't be caught dead with. But more important, if you *must* miss a meeting, the opening one probably is best for the purpose.

The Program Begins

Since conventions stick as closely to tradition as do church weddings, you can be fairly sure that your convention will open with an invocation, greetings from the association president to those hardy delegates who were able to get up in time for the session, and a welcome to the host city from some municipal dignitary, if it has always been done that way. Usually the mayor is slated for the job for big meetings, but since he seems to have as much difficulty arising in the morning as does the average citizen, it probably will be done by a member of the municipal PR department.

The succeeding opening formalities, unless your convention is an unusual one, will be no more day-brightening than the preceding activities. Frankly, they're not for a person suffering from a hangover or from a digestive system grumbling its way through a breakfast grabbed on the run.

Getting the Information

Right here it might be appropriate to pass on a tip which is not calculated to make you popular with those convention officials who rate their success on nose counts at each meeting. Unless your convention is very poorly run, you should be able to obtain printed copies of all addresses in the press room or at some other appointed spot. That's what many reporters do.

In many cases, copies are made available to interested people at the end of each convention session. A trip to the press room, however, will simplify matters for you, and keep you conveniently informed on meetings you accidentally (or deliberately) skip. This move may not endear you with the PR committee, but this is no time for timidity. You have rights as a paying delegate, exercise them.

Let's add right here that the foregoing is not offered as a substitute for meeting attendance, but rather as a supplement. There is nothing like getting your information from the horse's (in this case the speaker's) mouth. Treat the printed version as a permanent record of what you heard, or thought you heard.

What to Do When

At this time, even a mountain-sized hangover has passed away and you are ready for the serious work of the convention. At this point, if your convention follows a common pattern, you are likely to face a problem of selection.

Do you attend the afternoon meeting, or do you inspect the exhibits? If you're counting on the fact that the exhibits are open daily throughout the convention, forget it. Your choice won't be any easier tomorrow.

Most programs do list times for each session. So back to your program: Is the meeting an important one to you? Are all the subjects important to you, or none? If some are, what are they and where are they placed on the program? With a little luck, you may be able to catch those speeches you want to hear and still visit the exhibits. You can, that is, if your timing is good.

Now this is not quite so difficult as it may seem—just allow 40 minutes for each speaker and guide yourself accordingly. I know that some convention chairmen pride themselves on being able to arrange a program of short speeches, but don't count on it.

In the rare cases where a speech is short, it's invariably followed by one or more overlong ones. So, multiply the number of speeches by 40 minutes, keep a watch on your wristwatch, and do your roaming with a clear conscience.

The foregoing is a simplified version of the problem; very often it is complicated by a program arrangement which has two and even three meetings going on at the same time. There's no easy solution, but the approach to the problem is the same. And, as pointed out earlier, you can make use of printed copies of the speeches to keep informed.

The Exhibit Tour

Assuming that you are about to make the grand tour of the exhibits, this is a good time for some more foresight and careful planning. Every good convention provides a carefully coded and indexed layout of the exhibit floor. Get it, study it, determine where you want to go and exactly how to get there. It'll save a lot of backtracking.

There's room for difference of opinion as to when the exhibits can be most profitably toured. Our suggestion is a twofold one: Do your "shopping" early and once you have made up your mind, do your ordering later.

In the early stages, you will find the people manning each booth fresh, enthusiastic, and eager to talk about their product. You'll also find the competition for their attention keen. Later in the convention, you will find it easier to reach the person you want, who will have more time available. So look over products, pick up literature and take time to decide what you want to order before going back.

Your Speaker's Purpose

If, instead of the exhibit, your vote went to the afternoon meeting, don't waste it. LISTEN. Many convention speakers leave much to be desired, but they do have something to impart or they wouldn't be there. Do them, and yourself, a favor by not using this time to hold a heated conversation with the fellow in the neighboring seat.

Save your voice for the question and answer period which may close a session. Here is a real opportunity to benefit from the knowledge of your business compatriots. Take advantage of it, add your voice to the give and take.

With proper participation this give and take can be the most enjoyable, and profitable, part of the session. On the other hand, it can be a complete "bust" if everyone just sits and sits. If you have ever sat through a meeting where the buzz of conversation nearly drowned out a succession of hard-working speakers and then was succeeded by complete silence when a question from the floor was asked for, you'll understand what I mean.

Those Other Activities

The afternoon chores done, you are now ready, after a trip to your room for a shower and a short nap, for the tour of the hospitality suites.

Here, too, you have a choice: you can drift along with the crowd, taking what comes. Or you can proceed on a systematic basis of selection based upon the list you so carefully made out earlier, making your visits in the order of importance as you see it.

There is a third method of selection, based on information as to the size and quantity of shrimp being served. However, this is frowned on by many room-hoppers as unsportsmanlike. Take your shrimp as you find them, don't expect too much serious conversation, and you'll enjoy your evening.

Dining out or attending shows with your favorite suppliers and best friends is a must for many conventions. Often you only see the people once a year.

Take Mental Inventory

Along toward the final day, it might be wise to sit down and take a mental inventory. Have you accomplished everything you planned to do? Have you seen everyone you intended to? Do you have a complete set of notes, or papers, for your records?

One final suggestion: When you get home, take a long look at what you acquired in the way of knowledge, address your thanks in writing to those who warrant them (and your complaints to the sponsoring association's secretary or director), and start to rebuild your strength. Remember, there'll be another convention next year.

10

How to Remember Names and Faces

One of the prime skills that leads to success in business is the ability to get along with people. Our last chapter talked about attending conventions. Think where you might be if you didn't remember people. A good first step in this direction is to be able to remember who they are. Everybody likes to be thought important. When you forget a person's name or face, you say that you didn't think them important enough to learn who they are.

After all, you wouldn't forget Jimmy Carter or Ted Kennedy once you had met them. You certainly wouldn't forget somebody like Reggie Jackson. Remember, Joe Doe, Jean Smith, Tom Brown, or Salvatore Angelo are just as important —more important if they are customers or associates of one type or another.

Today, you can conquer this mental failing. Thousands of busy men and women are using certain tested principles to improve their memories, and they are finding that all it takes is the desire to remember plus some hard work.

Your Memory Can Be Improved

No matter how poor you feel your memory is, it can be made better. Experts tell us the memory is like a muscle. The more you exercise it, the more you strengthen it.

People have poor memories because they are too lazy to have good memories. Too many of us just barely observe

76

what is going on in the world around us. Scientists say that most of us are going around using less than a quarter of our full brainpower. Quick now, can you remember the numbers on the license plates on your car?

How to Sharpen Your Memory

When you visit customers or prospects at their businesses or homes, you find it easy to identify them because you expect to see them amid certain familiar surroundings. Even if you can't remember what they look like, there is little chance that this failing will embarrass you when you arrive.

But there is every chance that you might meet these same people unexpectedly on the street, at a restaurant, or at a meeting. With your points of reference gone, you could have a very offensive memory blackout. It might even cost you business.

Perhaps the one embarrassing moment that started me on the road to memory improvement began with my wife and me some years ago. We were trying to get a plane back home from Miami Beach during the height of the tourist season. In desperation I called a friend who was vice president of one of the large liquefied pertroleum gas companies in the area. He told me just to sit tight and he would get back to me. Less than a half-hour later we had our confirmed reservations.

Three months later I was sitting in the coffee shop of the Atlanta Biltmore Hotel with some other gas men who were attending a convention I was covering. A good-looking grey-haired man sitting across the room waved to me. I just couldn't place him, but I waved back anyway. After paying his check he walked by the table and said hello and asked about my wife. After small talk he left and I sat there hoping he hadn't noticed my confusion. Later I saw him across the lobby and asked the convention chairman his name. It was the man who had gone out of his way to arrange our plane

transportation. Right then and there I vowed to do everything I could to strengthen that lazy memory of mine.

One of the first things to do is to sharpen your powers of
observation. But remember one thing: unsystematic, helter-
skelter efforts rarely pay off. You must start to fill your
memory bank in a systematic manner.

Basically, the job is twofold: You must recognize the person's face or appearance, *and* remember his name. Your eye
is the key to recalling the face. Remembering his name
depends almost entirely on the sounds that reach your brain
through your ears.

Take Daily Mental Exercises

Specialists in memory improvement say that the first step is
to take daily mental exercises to stimulate your sluggish
memory. Here's a typical exercise. Shut your eyes and see if
you can visualize every detail of your office. Where is each
article located? How many shelves are there in the book-
cases? How many panes of glass in each window? How many
trade magazines are piled on your desk? Which magazine is
on top?

When you can recall all the details of your office, try other
less familiar rooms.

The second exercise will help improve your powers of
concentration. You can do this exercise at home tonight in
your favorite chair. See if you can recall everything you did
today. Whom did you talk to? About what? Where did you
eat? What did you have for lunch? If you had a luncheon
companion, what did he or she eat?

Another good test that will help make you the life of the
party is to concentrate on the funny stories and jokes you
hear during a meeting or a day's work. Sit down at night and
see how many you can remember.

Recognizing Faces

Several days of these mental calisthenics and you are ready to concentrate on the really big task of remembering people. There are six major steps to remembering faces. Here they are:

1. Be interested enough to want to remember the people you meet.

> After my embarrassing moment with the friend who had been able to arrange my transportation back from Miami Beach, I decided it was well worth my while to try to remember every person I would meet with whom I might have possible future contacts.

2. Look at the face.

> Get a general impression of the features. Study hair, eyes, nose, the shape of the head and ears, and other features or physical characteristics.

3. Find a special feature or characteristic to help you remember that person.

> For example: Bob Hope's ski-slope nose, Jimmy Carter's teeth, Winston Churchill's bulldog look, Jackie Gleason's bulk, Wilt Chamberlin's height.

4. Draw the face, either on paper or in your mind.

> You don't have to be an artist to use the outstanding feature to sketch a cartoon of the person you've just met. Actually, the cartoon is not really a picture. But because a cartoon can greatly exaggerate the special features of the person, it is easy to recognize him. If you've put the cartoon down on paper, don't be embarrassed. You don't have to show it to the person you've just met.

5. Compare the mental or drawn cartoon with this person the next time you see him or her.

6. Redo the cartoon after you've compared it with its model.

> You will find that your ability to make a picture (mental or actual) will increase with practice.

Another good exeircse along these lines is to stop for a few minutes and think about three or four good friends. What are their key features? Mentally cartoon them. Now practice with several fellow employees. If you want to see how good you can become, mentally cartoon the President, the mayor of your town, or some other noted person, so that you can check your own cartoon with those of the professional newspaper cartoonists.

Recalling That Name

Most of us have more trouble with names than with faces. This is because of the way we meet people. He is introduced to us, or else introduces himself. In either case, we hear the name and see the face. Usually, the name is given only once. However, we are able to continue to see and study the face. That's why the face is often all too familiar, but the name just evades us.

Memory experts offer a four-step program to help us recall names:

1. Get the name clearly and correctly.

Forget about looking over the person you are meeting, or thinking about what you were going to say until you have the full correct name engraved solidly in your mind. If the name is unusual or you failed to catch it, don't worry about hurting the person's feelings by asking that the name be repeated. In most cases, the person will be pleased that you think enough to get the name correct. You can bolster your recall by asking how the name is pronounced or spelled.

2. Use the name at once in your reply.

"I'm very happy to meet you, Ms. Gordon." Your new acquaintance has the chance to correct you if you have mispronounced her name. In any event, you've had the opportunity to further impress her name and face in your memory—and you've pleased her.

3. Repeat the name as often as possible in your conversation.

Each repetition fixes the name more firmly in your mind.

4. Write the name down as soon as you can.

Spelling it out on paper also acts to fix the name more firmly in your mind. Reread the name and practice pronouncing it. You might carry a small notepad or a sheet of paper for this purpose.

Association Is a Major Aid

You must make every effort to make certain you will not only remember your new acquaintance's face, but also the name that goes with it.

The experts say that the four rules we've just covered will help fix the name in your mind. Try connecting the name to one or more distinguishing factors, such as appearance, occupation, or something that will have a special meaning to you. This is what we call "association."

Very simply, association permits you to form a mental picture in your mind of a person and an object or idea in such a way that you will find it almost impossible to think of one without thinking of the other.

That is not as hard to do as it may sound. Many names have another real meaning in English. Many foreign names have meanings, too. It does take time and effort to form these associations. But practice will soon make the job easy.

In some cases making an association is quite simple. Mr. Silver may have a full head of white hair. Seeing him from a distance will telegraph his name to your brain.

There are many common words to which we can associate names. For example, there are the Blacks, Whites, Greys or

Grays, Greens or Greenes who associate to colors. Baker, Smith, Carpenter, Taylor, Wheelwright, and Shoemaker relate to occupations. We have Spring, Summers, March or May to go with the time of the year; or such adjectives as Strong, Strange, or Small.

There are many other names that have a definite meaning or are descriptive to us. Fox, Lyons, Rice, Rivers, or Lake are examples. Some people have the same name as a famous person and you can associate them with this person. The person could be a movie star, a sports figure, or a politician.

Those Difficult Names

Now, you may ask, "What about the more difficult names? The name that is not descriptive of anything?" The experts tell us to try to find an odd picture word that will jog our memory when we meet a person whose name falls into this category. If the word picture begins with the same letter, so much the better. Here are a few examples:

Altman—Alter
Berra—Beer
Chesnow—Chestnut
Diesman—Diamond
Serif—Syrup
Siegel—Seagull

Mr. Groshans might have big hands. Mrs. Nickel has a pleasant, round, almost coinlike face. How about Mr. Smith, the giant purchasing agent for the firm you've been trying to crack? You'll probably think of him as the big blacksmith who labored under the spreading chestnut tree, shoeing horses.

All this might sound ridiculous, but it isn't. These simple associations are often imaginary, but they do work. In fact, the more absurd your association, the more apt it is to work.

There is a good way to practice association. Look through a telephone book and select those names that have no meaning to you. Try to think up substitute names for these people. At first you might need a dictionary. After a little practice, this should be an easy game for you. Children do it all the time; most adults are just too lazy to try. You might try this as a car game the next time you take the family for a ride. Ask your children for the names of their classmates and see who can think up the best memory joggers for each name.

Just to review:

1. Try to visualize something with a meaning the same as the name.
2. If the name is the same as a famous person's, try to mentally picture the two together.
3. If there is no way to identify a person with a known something or person, find a word you can visualize that will help you to recall the name.

Meeting the Group

Now let's make it a little more difficult. Say you are attending a meeting or a convention. You walk into the hotel lobby or a suite and a friend calls you over to a crowd and calls out the names of everybody in his circle in rapid-fire succession. Most people would give up any attempt to remember each name and just grunt, "Pleased to meet you" to everybody.

But wait—remembering people you meet in a group is not really as tough as it seems. It does call, however, for harder work. Here are some of the ways to remember the names of people you meet in "large-size quantities" at gatherings.

1. Arrive early.

> This is one way to get a running jump on the future mob scene. You'll be able to wander about and meet people while they are still by themselves or are in smaller groups.

2. Get off in a corner by yourself for a few minutes and repeat those names you've already heard.

> Scan the group to see if you can identify each of those people you've met.

3. Slow down the introductions to make sure that you do get the name correctly.

4. Sit down as soon as you are home and go over the names of the people you have met and try to picture each one.

> This is a good time to put association to work for you.

5. Spend a few minutes during each of the next few days deliberately recalling the names of the people you met at the meeting.

Strengthening you memory calls for lots of hard work. But it is work that will pay dividends for you. You can remember names if you make the effort. Invest the necessary time to build your memory bank of names. It is one bank that will really pay off in satisfied customers and co-workers.

11
How to Profit by Listening

Unfortunately, listening is one gift which pays tremendous dividends that few of us really collect. We just don't listen as efficiently as we should.

In what other phase of your daily activities would you accept a 25 percent level of efficiency? Yet, that is the level of listening efficiency for most of us. You can really see the waste when you analyze your working day and find that you may spend 10 times as much time in listening as you do writing, up to five times as much as you do in reading, and from two to three times as much as you do in talking.

What's Hard About Listening?

Why is it so much harder to really listen than it is to read or write? For one thing, concentration in listening fights for attention against a feature peculiar to aural communication. The average rate of speech for most people is around 125 words per minute. This is considerably slower than your brain operates. What happens is that your brain has a good deal of spare time to loaf along or to devote to other subjects. This factor reduces the listening process of many people to a level of effectiveness far below what it really could be.

Listening Is an Art

Listening is really an art which offers several real benefits to you. First, as long as you are listening, you will profit in some way. You will learn something new, increase your present knowledge, or be entertained. Then, too, you gain the goodwill of other people. Generally, people prefer talking to listening. Every time you allow another person the opportunity to talk, he or she will become indebted to you.

There is a real danger, however, of permitting yourself to become a sounding board. In other parts of this book we've discussed how time can be wasted by idle chatter or gossip. Be as careful of lending your ear as you are of lending money.

What Causes Poor Listening?

For most of us, poor listening is caused by one or more of the following:

1. We are so busy trying to put our own ideas over that we don't bother to listen to what the other person has to say.
2. We are too lazy to listen. It is too easy to relax and just let the speaker's words flow right around us.
3. We fail to realize that we must make an effort to learn how to listen. And once we have achieved a good level of listening efficiency, we don't realize that we can only maintain it by staying in practice.

How to Hear More

Here are some suggestions which will help you to improve your listening efficiency. We'll elaborate on these as this chapter continues.

1. Think ahead of the speaker.
> Try to guess what he or she is leading up to. What conclusions will be drawn. In other words, try to anticipate what will be said.

2. Weigh the verbal evidence the talker presents to support his points.

3. Keep reviewing what the speaker says as your conversation continues.

4. Listen "between the lines."
> Search for the meanings the talker may not necessarily put into words. When people talk, words are only one part of their attempts to communicate with you. They use gestures and expressions which are supposed to be significant to you. Usually these nonverbal messages will strengthen what they have to say. Sometimes, however, they may contradict words. It is wise to watch these nonverbal actions because they sometimes may be more important than the words.

5. If you find it difficult to maintain your concentration at a 100 percent level while listening, stop the speaker and ask a question or two.
> The explanations will give you the opportunity to bring yourself back to full understanding. It will also assure you that you are getting a complete rundown of what you will be involved in.

6. You should practice concentration.
> Here's how: The next time you attend a meeting or convention, listen carefully to the speakers, but don't take notes. When they have finished, see if you can write a summary of what they said. Do the same when you listen to a speaker on the radio or television.

You might have your spouse or a friend read a speech or a newspaper editorial to you. When they finish, write a summary of what you've heard. This practice will help you step up your powers of concentration. And that calls for practice whenever you have the time.

Get the Point

When people talk to you, even informally, they usually try to make a point. Sometimes in the course of the talk they make several points, all of which add up to support their major position or idea.

A good listener tries to stay ahead of the talker by guessing what these points are before they are made. Whether you guess right or wrong, thinking like this pays off because you have forced yourself to concentrate so that you can analyze just what the talker is trying to tell you.

And, as mentioned earlier, you should also weigh and review what you have already heard. Such a review prevents your concentration from wandering. It is also wise to look for hidden meanings in what the other person is saying.

If you work at these mental activities, your ability to concentrate will certainly improve. And if it sounds like a lot of work, be assured that your normal thinking processes operate rapidly enough to provide you with ample time to perform all these mental tasks. Your mind is a wonderful instrument that can very rarely be overloaded.

Hear the Speaker Out

Another major obstacle to good listening is one which we may make ourselves. It is a reluctance to accept ideas different from our own that sometimes causes us not to listen.

The solution is to hear the speaker out. Withhold evaluation, judgment, and decision until after the speaker has finished. Then, and not before, review and make your assessment of the ideas. You should also hunt for the negative evidence—that is, ideas which might prove you wrong as well as those which prove you right. If you find yourself self-centered and inclined to consider others always wrong, you should force yourself to hear the other person out.

How to Profit by Listening

So much for building our understanding of the science of
listening. Let's take a look at how good listening can help
you in two of the most common phases of everyday business
life—buying and selling. I don't care if you are an engineer,
a research chemist, a school teacher, or a housewife; in one
way or another, you are involved in buying or selling.

As a customer or prospect, one of the most common
problems is that of protecting yourself against the high-
pressure "sales pitch." It may be a product, a service, or an
idea that you are exposed to. In such situations, the advantage
is generally the talkers' since they have at least three
points working in their favor:

1. **Time.**
    If you are reading, you can reread and take the time
    to reconsider. A sales talk usually requires a quick
    answer.
2. **An oral "sales pitch" is easier to give than a written one.**
    This is especially true because people usually don't
    listen to everything, and if their minds wander, they
    may unconsciously lower their sales resistance.
3. **Writers take greater pains with their words because their
words are down in black and white and can be checked and
double checked for accuracy.**
    In contrast, unless there is a tape recorder available, a
    talker can color words in any way he or she wishes.
    Exaggeration is a key tool of a high-pressure sales-
    person.

Two Types of Persuasion

You'll usually find that a person trying to sell you something
will use one of the two types of persuasive talks, or may even
make an attempt to combine them.

The first type is a low-pressure one, designed to allow you to think you will be able to make a choice after weighing the evidence. The speakers spread out both the facts for and against the proposal. As they conclude, they sum up and appeal for your support. If your listening is at peak efficiency, you can weigh the pros and cons of the proposal and make a decision.

Evaluation is much more difficult in the second type of persuasion. The speakers may not provide all the facts. They may use many emotion-arousing devices to place their story favorably before you. They may be unethical enough to leave out or misstate evidence. They may resort to name-calling, name-dropping, false testimonials, or a "band wagon" appeal.

To be fair, this second type could be for a worthy cause as well as for a bad one. The decision is entirely up to you. You do have a defense against this type of proposal. You should refuse to jump to conclusions, and request time to test the evidence. If you must say something immediately, let it be "No."

Four Tests for Evidence

There are four tests which you can give to the evidence presented in a persuasive speech. Try these to help you make your decision:

1. **The test of time.**
    Take a close look at the evidence if it is old and possibly outdated. What was right yesterday may not really be valid today.
2. **The test of competency of the source.**
    Make certain the talker knows what he or she is speaking about.
3. **The test of prejudice.**
    Is the speaker really neutral? Or more than likely prejudiced?

4. The test of completeness.
> Has the speaker given you all the facts? If not, why
> not?

How Listening Helps Selling

So much for your role as a buyer. Now, how can listening
improve your salesmanship? There are a number of ways in
which listening plays a part in the art of sales persuasion. If
you do a genuine job of listening, asking questions, and
listening to others, you will actually be putting yourself in
the other person's shoes. This is one of the key reasons for
the success of most salesmen. If the customer feels that you
know and understand needs and problems, he or she will be
definitely more friendly toward you.

On the simplest level, listening can serve as a means of
learning the customers' needs and problems in relation to
what they want to buy or are going to be asked to buy.

The "listen before you act" approach to selling is built
around a central question: How can you sell yourself or your
product if you don't know what the prospective buyer wants
and needs? This is a very simple premise. Unfortunately, it
still remains unrecognized by many who sell.

Don't Stop Listening

You should never cease your aural study of the people with
whom you must deal. As they talk, you should note with care
both what they say and what they don't say. The way they
skirt an objection may reveal their true feelings. So keep
looking beyond the mere content of what you hear.

Properly used, the skill that is listening will be a strong tool
to help you achieve success.

12
Thinking Your Way to the Right Decision

You can think your way to greater success in your business and in your everyday life. The key is simply to train your mind to utilize the creative potential you possessed when you were born and to use a simple six-step formula you'll find later on in this chapter.

The ability to think straight is an important asset to any person who must make decisions. And decision making is not limited to businessmen and women. You make decisions every single day of your life—choosing new clothes, buying a home or car, joining a club, going to a show, or choosing what to have for dinner.

There is a definite map to making decisions, but before we examine it, let's take a look at the thinking process. We can define "thinking," for our purposes, as the careful and diligent efforts to discover methods of resolving the difficulties that face us in the everyday course of our lives.

Making decisions would, of course, be much less of a chore if you could be sure that your decisions would not kick back. It is fear of failure, the consequence of guessing wrong, that often makes the decision-making process such an ordeal. Yet, this emotional strain can be reduced if you have a better understanding of what a decision is and if you learn how to protect your decision against failure.

Two Kinds of Decisions

Most of us in our everyday work deal with two kinds of decisions. We could call them the routine and the major decisions. In the routine, the conditions of the situation and the requirements which the solution has to satisfy are known to us. Our job is simply to choose between a few obvious alternatives. The basis for our judgment is often economy; and the decision is one that will accomplish the goal with a minimum of effort and disturbance.

Major decisions are something very different. They involve us to the extent that we must either find out what the situation is or change it—either finding out what the resources are or what they should be. Among your major decisions are those affecting productivity of a business, revamping an organization, large capital expenditures, training of salesmen and others, realignment of routes or districts, plant layout, and the flow of paperwork through an office.

In major decisions the important job is not so much to find the right answer as to find the right question. There is nothing so useless as the right answer to the wrong question.

It is not enough to find the right answer. The course of action decided on must be put into effect. Management of a business, a club, or a home is not concerned with knowledge, but with performance. Nothing is so wasted as the answer which goes nowhere or the solution that is sabotaged by the people who could make it effective.

Dealing with Unknowns

No system can ever lead you inevitably to a correct decision; you'll always face unknown or unanticipated elements. Suppose you are the sales manager of a company and you select from a group of job applicants a very promising candidate for training in a key position. Your choice proves to be enthusiastic and eager, and everything moves nicely for the next few months. Then his wife inherits a large sum from an unexpected source and wants him to go into business for himself. Your months of training go out the window.

Let's find another example at the housewives' level. Say you are P.T.A. president and assign responsibility for a special event to a woman who has always done hard work in her committees. Unbeknownst to you, her husband is expecting a transfer and a promotion. Since this woman expects to be gone by the time your event rolls around, she unconsciously slows down and does very little planning. Just before your event, she moves and you are left holding the bag.

There was nothing wrong with either of these appointments, even though later developments proved them to be "wrong." You can never anticipate all eventualities. But within the limits of chance, you can improve your decision-making score—and with it your willingness to make decisions and to be decisive in all matters.

Three Rules of Decisiveness

The most important rule in decision making is to act decisively. Decisiveness is a habit which may be acquired if you follow these three rules religiously:

1. Decide all the small matters promptly.
2. Select your decision and forget the alternatives.
3. Put your decision into action.

Very rarely will you be asked to make decisions impulsively. But don't be afraid to make a mistake. Right or wrong, make a decision as soon as you have pursued the process of reaching a decision. And whatever decision you make should be a valid one, not merely an escape from the responsibility of making a decision.

Many a decision made from sheer fright is just a wild grasp in any direction. A man who has held back from making a decision until conditions just won't let him procrastinate any longer may find that the best solutions are no longer open to him. He may also find that he must now act without being able to give proper consideration to his problem.

The Decision-Making Process

A formula for making decisions was mentioned earlier. Here are the six steps that make it up.

1. Properly identify the problem.
2. Gather all available data.
3. List all possible solutions.
4. Test all possible solutions.
5. Select the best solution.
6. Put your decision to work.

After you analyze these six simple steps you will see that most of your past attempts at decision making have included these six basic actions, whether you realized it or not. You probably just didn't give the right names to what you have been doing. These six steps are normally followed in the order given, though the sequence can vary. Often you are already gathering data while you are trying to isolate the big problem. At other times you will be working on more than one phase at a time.

Properly Identify the Problem

What appears at first glance to be the elements of the problem seldom are the really important or relevant things. They are at best symptoms, and often the most visible symptoms are the least revealing ones.

A clash of personalities may be the result of poor organizational structure. An apparent problem in manufacturing costs may really be an engineering mistake or one in sales planning.

The first chore, then, is to find the real problem and to define it. This is not a matter for haste, but for careful inspection and deliberation. Definition of the problem cannot be accomplished until the element or elements are found in the situation which must be changed or acted upon.

Actually, you are halfway to a solution when you can write out a clear statement of your problem. This is often a tough job in business because few problems appear in truly clear-cut form. For example, suppose you find production behind schedule in your plant. You also know that you have been plagued with many absences. What is your real problem? Is it cutting absenteeism, or are the absences a sign of low employee morale? When you've carefully analyzed your problem, you may find it is "how to raise employee morale," not "how to improve production" that needs attention.

Careful study is necessary if you are to define properly your real problem. Sometimes you'll discover that the major problem is really made up of several smaller ones. These should be isolated and treated individually.

When you have found your real problem, write it down in as simple a way as possible. This will now act as a guide to help you keep your mental processes on the right track. Once this is done, you are ready for the next step.

Gathering All Available Data

The next step requires you to collect all the information you can that pertains to your problem. Obtain every possible fact and figure that is available. You will rarely see a person who has all the facts make a mistake because he or she knows too much.

Suppose you decide you want to take up golf. You'll want to know where you can play, where and how you can learn to play, what equipment and lessons will cost you, what other expenses you could have. With this information on hand, you will then go ahead and decide if you want to pursue the hobby.

You should organize your collection of facts into some form that will permit you to make sense of them. One of my business friends carefully lists each fact on a separate file card before starting the decision-making process. He then discards those cards he feels will not provide an answer. Another man rules a sheet of paper in half the long way and lists the facts on the left side. As he studies each, he notes its relative importance and meaning on the right side.

Both the cards and the list are simply ideas for small businesses or for everyday family use. In larger businesses and corporations, charts, graphs, and reports are made up to help with the decision.

One of the best ways to gather reliable data is to get out in the field and see what is going on for yourself. An oil distributor was faced with the problem of low gallonage delivered per truck mile. It took him only one morning to find out the reason for his problem.

He learned that his drivers loaded their tank trucks in the morning, using the time the fuel oil was being pumped into the tanks to gossip. About an hour after they finally left the plant, they all met at a diner for coffee and a chance to chew the fat some more.

The solution was the institution of a new rule that all tank trucks must be filled every night. A morning and an afternoon coffee break were allowed, but each driver was to call in on his two-way radio when he was taking the break and let the dispatcher know where he could be reached. The long hauls over to the favorite diner were ended by the rule that coffee breaks were to be taken at the eating place closest to the last delivery.

Knowledge of the facts permitted a simple and profitable solution to the problem.

List All Possible Solutions

We start getting creative when we develop possible solutions to the problem that faces us. Here is where you should let your imagination have free reign to seek and offer new ideas to you. It is wise to write down every solution you come up with before you start to analyze and discard. Even if an idea seems absurd, write it down.

It is amazing how many ideas you can develop to fit any one problem once you've set your mind to it. I attended a seminar on creative problem solving at the University of Buffalo some years ago. Each of the group was asked to reveal a personal or business problem that was bothering him. The others would "brainstorm" and offer solutions.

One of the youngest in my group was the son of a wealthy dairy owner. After training summers in different departments at the dairy, he was to start working full time in an executive position when he finished college. He was concerned that there would be friction when he moved in and the old-timers suddenly faced a new "unbeatable" rival.

Our group "brainstormed" 96 different ideas to help that young man!

You won't have a group to help you, but this is an example of the many possible solutions that can exist for a particular problem.

How long should you gather and study data? Only as long as you can get something new from the information you have.

An added tip: After you have carefully analyzed all the facts and listed your possible solutions, sleep on them! You can do this by actually shutting up shop for the day and going home, or you can shift to another project that is completely different for an hour or two. Come back in a few hours or the next morning to choose the solution or solutions to be tested.

Test All Possible Solutions

You must try to be as objective as possible when you are testing the solutions you've come up with. If you are not truly objective, you may put aside judgment and select a solution you particularly favor, even if it is the wrong one. One way to help yourself be objective is to measure each solution against a guidepost or yardstick.

Each of your solutions could be studied in the light of the following:

1. Will this solution solve our problem?
2. Will this be a permanent or a stopgap solution?
3. Will the solution work in actual practice?
4. How much will the solution cost?
5. Can I, or the company, afford the cost?
6. Will all affected people go along with the solution?

Select the Best Solution

The true job of an executive is to make the final decision. It is a decision you have to live with and sleep with. Occasionally, one solution will stand out head and shoulders above the rest. If this is the case, you are lucky.

Sometimes, however, you may find that no one solution has come through all of your tests with a passing grade. The best choice may actually be a marriage of two or more of your solutions. Here you must gather together the strongest points of each of the solutions that will be used. Use your imagination together with your innate management skills to make the final decision.

Another word of advice here. The greatest problem is the temptation to let thinking be guided by desires or emotions. The following seven rules will help you keep your thinking logical:

1. **Avoid quick decisions.**
    Refuse to accept any solution until you have arrived at it by a step-by-step process.
2. **Eliminate any emotional influences as much as possible.**

3. Relax your mind, because you come up with distorted views and tend to take short cuts when you work under heavy pressure.

4. Study again any one solution or decision that seems too much in line with your own wishes.

5. Double check your first solution to see if it really is the proper one.

6. Think and think some more about your problem and its ramifications so that you do not take impulsive action.

7. Understand that the facts must be followed, even if the decision will be one that is distasteful.

Put Your Decision to Work

"Scientific" decision making has one last stage—putting your decision to work. If it works perfectly, you know you've made the right decision.

If the problem doesn't disappear after you've made all allowances for any unforeseen difficulties, you'll have to go back through the decision-making process again. Perhaps now that you have seen what difficulties arise, another of your solutions will stand out as a better one.

Be absolutely certain that you did not define the wrong problem. Earlier it was said that the important key was to pick the right problem. Your choice could have been unsuccessful only because it was developed for the wrong problem.

People Are Most Important

Remember, no decision can be any better than the people who have to carry it out. A course of action may require more competence and understanding than the people involved may have, and yet be the only possible solution. If this is the case, you must provide in your decision for the efforts needed to raise the ability and standards of the present staff, or else find the new people who do have what it takes.

A perfect home-front example can be found in my own religious congregation. A major problem was to gain sufficient publicity for the group's events and programs. Finally, the secretary checked over the membership cards and found that several men including myself were in public relations work. We were invited to come to a special meeting and offer advice. We quickly entered into the overall planning and promotion of all activities. It was a release and hobby for us. If we hadn't been asked to help, we would probably have never considered offering our services.

As a decision maker you can define, classify, assemble, set objectives, and select the solution, but you cannot supply the one ingredient needed to convert a solution into a decision—*action*. You only can communicate to others what they should be doing and motivate them to do it. And only as they take the right action is the decision actually made.

The participation of others in preliminary phases of decision making may not be necessary and in some cases is actually undesirable. In many other instances, the people charged with carrying out the decision should take part in the work of developing alternatives. This may help in the final decision, because they can spot hidden difficulties and uncover overlooked resources which they know about because of their closeness to the solution.

And as a final suggestion: Because the decision affects the work of others, it must help them achieve their objectives, assist them in their work, and contribute to their performing more effectively and with a greater sense of achievement. Decisions cannot be merely for the maker's benefit and satisfaction.

Modern business makes it highly important that every manager understand the process of decision making. You should understand these tools and their limitations, and also when to call on outside assistance.

Once you understand the basic methods involved in decision making, you will find yourself less likely to resort to gimmicks. Straight thinking will help you chart the right course in the uncertain sea of business competition, which is getting rougher for the unskilled with every advance of technology.

13
How to Profit from Your Mistakes

Running a business provides many opportunities for making mistakes. To be really successful, a businessman must be decisive rather than cautious. We discussed this in the last chapter.

In today's highly competitive world, the one who delays or fears to act has made an even bigger error than the one whose decision went wrong. But the successful people are the ones who try to do something about a mistake. They must admit to errors. More important, they must undo them whenever possible and profit from these errors.

First, recognize that a mistake does not mean the end of the world. Realize that failure comes because of:

1. Misjudgments
2. Imperfect planning
3. Inadequate implementation.

How to Undo Mistakes

Second, act to undo the mistake and see that it does not happen again. In most cases this calls for a four-part program:

1. Analyze your mistake.
2. Consider the cause or causes.

3. Prepare new plans of action.
4. Seek to benefit in some way from your error.

Analyze Your Mistakes

Before you can do anything about your mistake, it must be analyzed from your first idea to your last action. This will help you find out just why you lost out. Here are some guideposts for error analysis.

1. Was the error really important?
2. How was the error made?
3. Can you be certain the error will not recur?
4. Had your plans been really suitable for the project?
5. Was the timing of your action suitable?
6. Had you anticipated all eventualities?
7. Did you make an effort to check progress?
8. Did you have the right personnel to do the job?
9. Did your people have the proper information?
10. Did your people have the proper tools?
11. Did you or another adequately supervise your plan?
12. Was communication between all parties satisfactory?
13. Was the project completely followed up so that all data available was obtained?
14. Was top management 100 percent behind the plan of action?
15. Was the action one that was stopgap?
16. Was the action one that was overly favored by you over other courses of action?

Consider the Cause

There are many reasons for errors. These include the lack of information, carelessness, misunderstanding, poor communications, and acts of God. Three oil distributors I know are perfect examples of having met these causes. Heavy investments in bulk storage and new delivery equipment became a financial hardship to one because unseasonably warm weather wrecked a heating season.

Another distributor invested heavily in two new service stations, only to find that the highway commission decided to build an alternative route. This was simply an error of carelessness through his failure to seek information on new road construction plans.

A third jobber assigned a ne'er-do-well brother-in-law to the management of one of his branches. He knew the man drank and was undependable, but agreed to the move to soothe his wife. Within six months many customers were alienated, employees' morale was nonexistent, and the till had been tapped to make up gambling losses.

Prevent Recurring Errors

Once you've made the analysis, make certain that you act to prevent your error from happening again at some future time. When you have satisfied yourself that you know all the reasons for failure, you are ready to take the next step. This is insurance that the error or similar ones will not recur. If possible, try to set up a procedure that guarantees permanent elimination of the trouble.

For example, the man who mislocated the service stations should make certain he has all sources of information about road-building plans for the future. The man who over-financed storage and delivery equipment could seek better credit terms or methods of financing in the future.

We all know that the distributor with in-law trouble should exercise closer control over his hiring, but just how do you placate your spouse unless you really put your foot down? If he is forced to hire the wrong man (such as a brother-in-law) again, he must put the man in a position that will not affect

the people who are important to the business—both customers and employees. He should also plan to maintain a
closer watch over the relative's actions.

In general, the reason for the mistake or error dictates the
action. If an employee is involved, additional training could
be an answer. Unanticipated developments can be kept to a
minimum if safeguards are set up to provide warning signals.
A system of rechecking can also be set up.

Action After the Error

Once you know all the facts, you are ready to admit your
mistake and to make new plans to run your business or to do
your job. At this time it might be well to digress a moment
and look at the position of employees who have made a
mistake. This would be employees at the management or
supervisory level.

Once they clearly understand why and how the error
happened, they should admit their error. Those who don't
may soon find themselves involved in a maze of lies from
which they cannot extricate themselves.

There is a definite factor in your favor. Admission of an
error does not have to be done in a negative manner. All
employees should take advantage of what they have learned
from the error to transform their report into a constructive
one.

They should think in terms of their boss's reaction. They
should not waste the boss's time with long, involved reports
about why an error happened. They shouldn't overplay their
anguish about making a mistake.

Very simply, one person who works for another should
realize that the boss wants to know that something has
happened that has caused certain other actions, and that the
employee has taken steps to solve the problem. The report
should be brief and factual.

Reevaluating Programs

When you are satisfied that you fully understand the reason for the failure, it's time to act. First decide if you want to repeat the action or program. Can you use the same approach or one only slightly revised? In any case, your analysis of failure will point out which weak spots must be strengthened if the program is to be reused or modified.

Secondly, the reasons for the error may show that substantial changes must be made in the plan. You may have to consider firing some people and hiring new personnel. It might be necessary to purchase new equipment. New methods of operation, new procedures, or revised timing may also be dictated.

Salvaging Poor Actions

There is a third alternative to either repeating or revising your earlier programs: a salvaging operation to prevent your first program from becoming a complete loss. After all, any action you did take has paid off at least by what you have learned from it.

What you have learned from your error or mistake can be used to point up weaknesses in your operations. Eliminate these, and your experiences will pay off in knowledge invaluable in your future decision-making actions.

Taking New Action

Now you are ready to move your business or your career ahead to new profits and greater success. This calls for several policy-making actions.

1. Take a new look at your goals and purposes.
2. Search for new techniques.
3. Make your new plans.
4. Look for the bugs in your new plans.
5. Assign the proper people to the job.
6. Prepare a definite schedule.
7. Start your new plan rolling.
8. Follow up to see that the plan is working properly.
9. Revise or modify your plan as necessary.

Never Ignore Mistakes

The most important rule for errors is that they should never be ignored. Despite the irritations and frustrations of failure, mistakes, and errors, remember that the ability to benefit from these setbacks can lead to greater success. Careful analysis of the failure points out the areas of weaknesses and often reveals unknown strengths. You can profit from failure by asking such questions as:

1. Can the causes of failure be eliminated?
2. What ideas, experiences, or techniques can be salvaged from the mistake?
3. Does the failure provide evidence of other activities that should be re-examined?

Make certain that all facts affecting the failure and the causes are studied and measured. If the errors are just forgotten, they will grow larger. No matter what the mistake is or whatever the circumstances affecting it are, the failure must be subjected to the same careful analysis that precedes any decision.

It is taken for granted that each of us will err at some time. Your success is really rated on what you do to undo your mistakes and to profit from them.

14
The Art of Trouble Shooting

Our historians have always managed to assign a name to a period of time. They have come up with such graphic ones as "Dark Ages," "Renaissance," and "Industrial Revolution." In the future they will probably label our own era "The Aspirin Age." We seem to be a race beset by problems in our business and everyday life. It has been said that we down more than 10,000,000 pounds of aspirin every year as a result of these problems.

In Chapter 12 we discussed decision making. There is no doubt that every problem requires that we make a decision as we attempt to ease our worries. But not all actions requiring decisions are problems, even though many decisions saddle us with problems. Our social and business environments continually breed problems that require fast action. These may be problems in dealing with people, with equipment, or with products or services. Our success in solving these problems can be helped by the simple problem-solving formula that follows in this chapter.

Caution: Separate Worry from Problems

Worry can be defined, for our purposes, as a combined physical and emotional tension that creeps over a person who is perplexed. To solve a problem quickly, you must first overcome worry. For too many of us, worry acts as a substitute for figuring things out. It is the deadly enemy preventing us from thinking straight.

You can overcome worry if you form strong mental patterns that will take over automatically and begin to solve each problem as it occurs. If you achieve this, your built-in problem-solving habit should take over one-two-three just as automatically as when you slide behind the wheel of your car and instinctively begin to drive.

Prevention Is the First Step

The easiest way to solve a problem is to try to prevent it from happening in the first place. If you want to prevent trouble with your house, your car, or your heating unit, you see that these items are checked and receive good service. In a business this is called preventive maintenance.

Problem-Solving Formula

The formula for decision making had six steps; there are four in the formula that will help you act fast as a troubleshooter of your problems:

1. Get all the facts and define your problem.
2. Weigh the facts and decide what to do.
3. Act on your solution.
4. Measure your success.

Define Your Problem

The first step is to define and clarify your problem so you'll know exactly what you are trying to solve. Just suppose you are driving and your car stops dead. You look first at the gauges in your dashboard, and you discover that you are out of gasoline. All you have to do is to find a way to refuel your car. But suppose you have plenty of gas. Now you have to look further to find out why your car will not run.

The more facts you have, the easier your problem solving will be. You can handicap yourself if you try to solve your problem before you have a sufficient understanding of what is going on. So step number one, again, is to get the facts . . . *all* the facts.

Weigh the Facts

You must have the complete story so that you can review the problem and see what rules or policies apply, and talk it over with other people if necessary. With these facts well in hand, you are ready for step number two.

All the facts and information you have gathered must be made to fit together, or else be discarded. You now weigh each fact in your mind and come up with one or several possible courses of action.

Many times there will be more than one possible solution. Here your past experience comes in handy. Follow the action suggested by what has most often proved successful in the past.

If you can find no action that has been successfully used before, you must consider carefully the possible effect of every possible solution on all people involved.

What you have actually done is pieced all the facts together, considered their relationship with each other, checked to find precedents, decided what to do, and tried to estimate the effects of your actions on your business or environment, on other people involved, and on you yourself.

Act on Your Solution

With your groundwork completed and your decision made, you are ready to put your solution into action. The assembly and consideration of all the facts, the weighing of the facts, and the actual decision are merely motions that accomplish nothing until you actually put your solution to work.

The action may involve only you, or you may need the assistance and participation of others. If you were going to act to have a neighbor remove a fence from your property, for example, you would need the help of a lawyer.

Even when you decide to act and start the ball rolling yourself and then utilize the assistance of an expert, such as a lawyer, you have not completed the problem solving until you have decided who will do the necessary work, how much each will do, and when each will do what is expected of him.

Measure Your Success

Even now you are not finished. You still have to complete what is probably the most important step in our trouble-shooting operation. You must check the results of your action. If everything is moving along, fine! If the problem still exists to some degree, you must completely re-examine the whole solution and find out what went wrong, or just what you failed to do.

Your follow-up should begin almost immediately after you put a solution to work. This follow-up should be a continual process until you are firmly convinced that you have solved your problem. If you are dealing with people, you will have to watch their actions closely.

A man or woman who can trouble shoot will quickly gain the reputation of a person who can be counted on. If you are working for somebody else, your boss will realize your abilities and potentials and your advancement should be assured. If you have your own business, those who supply you merchandise and products, the bankers who supply your money needs, and the friends and neighbors who need help and guidance in community activities will all come to respect you and look to your leadership.

WORKING WITH OTHERS

15
How to Be a Good Communicator

From the president of a nation or a business on down, communication is the primary job of every man or woman who aspires to success of any sort.

If you want to get things done, the key to your success is the ability to use that all-important tool—communication. As much as 80 to 90 percent of an executive's time is spent giving or receiving ideas, instructions, decisions, or plans, and trying to obtain understanding.

Communication can be accomplished in two ways: through the spoken word and by writing. This chapter will cover the basic principles of communication as well as the art of speaking face-to-face. The following chapters will examine effective writing techniques and the preparation and delivery of speeches and talks.

Communication Skills Must Be Developed

Too many of us take communication for granted. We devote countless hours to developing our skills in accounting, management, or science, or in learning to play golf. But we do not take the time to develop our communication skills, even though our very success will depend upon how well we communicate.

There is no magic to learning how to be a good communicator. You know what ideas you want to communicate to others. Your problem is to find the proper words to say what you want to say so that others understand what you want them to do.

Organize Yourself

The first step to getting your ideas across is to know in advance what you want to say. You must organize your thoughts before you say anything. Then carry your instructions or descriptions logically from one point to the next. Carefully tie your different ideas together so that the people you are talking to are never confused.

If you think it easy to give an instruction to other people, try this simple test I saw conducted at a meeting of the Sales Executive Club of New York. Two men were invited up to the stage. One was stationed on one side of a curtain; the other stood on the other side and was supposed to tell his partner how to draw a not very complicated collection of straight lines. The audience was able to see the progress made by the "artist." It was amazing to see how difficult it was for the "instructor" to describe just what he wanted the "artist" to do. The finished drawing did not at all resemble the original.

To communicate, you must underline in your own mind the important thoughts that you wish to pass along in this meeting with other minds. Then you use every technique you can to achieve your objective.

One last suggestion here. Don't try to throw too many different ideas into one communication. It may confuse the other person, or give the impression that you are quite confused.

Don't Preach When You Talk

Few people like to be talked at or talked down to. They want to be talked *to* as an equal. You can put your ideas across most forcefully and without arousing resentment if your tone is both courteous and considerate.

Use All Your Tools

When you are talking face-to-face, there are many little things you can use to put over what you want to say. These are simple techniques that you should put to work for you. They include your facial expressions, your eye movements, and the tone of your voice. Your choice of words and their "finer" meanings will also help you obtain the reactions you wish.

And speaking of tone, put pep into what you want to say. The flat lackluster tone of voice that moves stolidly along may very well put your listeners to sleep, because they give up trying to pick out the important points that you are trying to make. If you want to emphasize an important idea, raise your voice or lower it, whichever is necessary to underline vocally what you believe is important.

Try and Try Again

Suppose you can't seem to put your idea across. The answer is to try again another way. Adjust your methods to your listener. Your manner of speaking may even vary. You'll talk one way if you are trying to explain a problem, another if you are asking for information, and still a third way if you are giving a direct order.

You should try to pick the right words—those that will be understood by the person with whom you are speaking. If the other person fails to understand you, both of you are wasting time. Your objective is to use the words that mean the same things to both of you.

If you are not certain that you are getting across, repeat yourself. But try to say it another way. You might use an illustration or two to strengthen your original presentation.

Give as Well as Take

Don't do all the talking. Give the other person a chance to respond to you. Try to encourage the others who are listening to participate by slanting your conversation in such a way that they have to contribute. You can ask them questions. You can ask for suggestions. You can ask for their experience. When you express your interest in them, you can usually get them to take part wholeheartedly.

Try to give the other person some idea or benefit from your presentation. Look at everything from the other person's point of view and show how he or she will benefit by doing what you suggest. And remember, it is just as vital to do this with people who work for you as it is with people at your own level or above.

Try Listening

Some of us have a bad fault. We forget that communication is a two-way street. It's more than just getting the other person to take part in the conversation. Some of us just stop listening when others open their mouths.

You must be attentive to your listener's every action. Watch faces, eyes, body movements. You can quickly discover if you have lost the listener's interest. And you must then listen to what is said in response and how it is said. When you discover how the other person is receiving your message, you'll be better able to put the emphasis on your words to put your message over.

When to Stop Talking

Once you finish, stop talking. Never underestimate the intelligence of the other person. If you continue to repeat yourself and your ideas, you take the chance of losing your listener's interest in your proposal, as well as the other person's attention. The rule is to say it simply, say it fast, and shut up.

The Follow-Up Is Vital

The most expert communicator can fail if he or she does not follow-up. Even under the most ideal circumstances, your thoughts may not be understood. Most people are just unable to absorb all of what they hear or read.

Your big problem is to find out just how much of what you say to other people is understood. The only way to be certain that your suggestions or orders are carried out is to ask them to repeat what you said. Ask as many questions as necessary to let you know that they understood what is expected. If they are doing a job for you, you can review their performance to see just how well you have been understood.

Psychologists tell us that the best way to make an impression on another person is to appeal to as many senses as you possibly can. One of the best ways to put your ideas over is to use visual aids to reach others through their eyes. You don't have to have expensive visual aids made up. A simple sketch or diagram, or even a photograph, will reinforce your oral instructions.

Your Voice Is Also a Tool

It may be possible that while your words are well chosen and your ideas easily understandable, you are not getting your story across for another reason. Your voice may be against you. It may be irritating or distracting to the people with whom you are communicating.

Stop for a second and analyze just what a voice means to you when you are listening to somebody else. Does a weak, hesitant voice indicate weakness or lack of confidence? Does a harsh voice give you the impression that the other person is arrogant and one you could dislike? Is the firm, cultured voice indicative of a confident, poised speaker?

Into which of these categories do you fall?

There is an easy way to find out, and you may be surprised at the results, because few of us actually would recognize our own voice if we heard it as others do. The best way to study your own voice is to obtain a tape recorder and to let it run while you are talking on the phone or to another person. Now play the recorder back. Do you note any of the following defects?

1. A slurring or mumbling of words, or
2. A lack of expression with a lapse into a monotone, or
3. An unpleasant tone that may be too high, nasal, or breathless, or
4. A lot of word pauses such as *oh . . . ah . . . mmm*, or other similar sounds.

Ask another person who is interested in you to sit down and listen to the tape. It may be your spouse, an associate, or a good friend. Ask this person to be frank and tell you what he or she really thinks.

You may find that you will need a speech teacher or expert to help improve your voice. Speech improvement assistance is available from many sources. Colleges, universities, and even high schools offering adult education courses offer speech classes. In many localities, organizations such as the Sales Executive Clubs run similar classes. There are also specialists who can be hired to help you. Many people have joined local chapters of the Toastmaster organizations. Here they get the opportunity to practice their speech and to have others with similar problems offer constructive criticism.

Speaking Rate Must Be Regulated

We can offer some tips to help you speak with greater clarity. Find the proper rate of speed that for you will ensure intelligible speech. If you speak too rapidly, you may slur your words. In contrast, a slow, steady rate of speed quickly becomes a monotone. Good speakers vary their speed as they talk. They often emphasize important points by pausing both before and after the major thought.

If you talk in a tone too low or too high, your listeners may become annoyed. It will definitely be distracting. When you talk to others, it's wise to pitch your voice at the same level they are using. Vary this pitch for emphasis so that you make it easier for them to listen to you and, therefore, to understand you.

The skills of oral communication can be improved through practice just as you can improve your golf game or your swimming. Once you have achieved the ability to communicate effectively, you have gone a long way toward assuring yourself both that you can get others to do what you want, and that you will be able to put your point of view over at all times.

16
Say It Simply
When You Are Writing

Living and working in today's world, you receive and write more letters, memos, and reports than your counterpart did 20 or more years ago. And all this writing can come back to haunt you at some future time. In speaking, your actual words virtually disappear into the air. In writing, however, anyone who wishes to can save what you have written for future reference. Writing, therefore, plays a big role in the continued growth of every one of us.

You don't have to be a professional writer to compose good letters, memos, and reports with a minimum of time and effort. But many executives seem to tense up when faced with the prospect of writing. They know what they want to say, but the process of putting their thoughts on paper seems to frighten them.

I hope that the simple rules I'll outline in this chapter will help make business writing easier for you.

Secure Favorable Response

First of all, remember that the basic purpose of any business message is to secure a favorable response from those to whom it is directed. If your message does not gain this goal, it is worthless, regardless of the time and effort you spend composing it.

A second fact to bear in mind is that your readers' time is very valuable, whether they are associates, superiors, suppliers, customers, or your subordinates.

Third, remember that you must write your message so that there is no possibility for you to be misunderstood. You can do this if you remember that any communication can be effective if it is accurate, is well planned and thought out in advance of writing, and is clear and brief.

Here are four sound rules worth remembering:

1. **Don't say anything unless you can back it up with facts.**
   Inaccuracies will reflect upon your ability.
2. **Plan your communication before you begin to write.**
   Think out your idea. Assemble all needed data and arrange it in logical importance.
3. **Write simply.**
   Many people think that by using semilegal or impressive-sounding phrases they are giving the impression of education and importance. Nothing could be farther from the truth. These words tend to slow the reader down, and may often make it more difficult to understand what is wanted. Why say "hereafter and henceforth" when "in the future" is clearer? Why use "due to the fact that" when one word, "since," will suffice?
4. **The importance of being brief is obvious.**
   If you follow the three previous rules, there will be no need for repetition. Excessive wordage should be eliminated so that you save both your own and your reader's time.

The good writers are known for their brevity. For example, the Gettysburg Address contains only 266 words. The Ten Commandments comprise 297 words. The Declaration of Independence has only about 1,500 words.

There are two good rules to remember. First, before you take a pen in hand or begin to dictate to your secretary, ask yourself: "Is this message necessary? Do I have anything to say?"

If you must write, then, second: "Can I find a briefer, clearer way to say what I want to say?"

Writing the Business Letter

Successful executives budget their time and schedule certain of their activities for a definite time period of the day. Part of your daily schedule should include a time when you read your incoming mail, and a specific time for answering it.

Many prefer to give their mail some thought before they answer it. This is advisable. They read their correspondence in the morning and dictate their replies in the afternoons.

As you read your mail, it may be advisable in some cases to jot down important points in the margin of the letter. This might include such matters as what information to have your secretary look up so that you can give an intelligent answer.

In planning your letter, you won't go wrong if you follow the excellent guide to good writing that has been established by our newspaper editors. They insist that their reporters tell them: who, what, when, where, why, and how.

Another important point to remember is the tone of your communication. Too often, people in business forget that their major stock in trade is their friendliness. You should try to make your friendly attitude readily apparent to your readers. You can do this as you write or dictate by thinking of the recipient as your friend. Not only will a friendly letter create a better impression with your readers, it will help place them in a receptive frame of mind.

The Mechanics of Writing

Too many executives are overly concerned with the mechanics of writing. Good English is important and you should strive for correct usage, or else you show your ignorance or laziness. But there is no reason to become a slave to grammatical perfection. Some men and women become so involved that they pay more attention to periods, commas, and semicolons than they do to the message they are trying to communicate.

But it is nonetheless advisable to take a very brief look at the "signposts" that direct our language.

To begin with, the semicolon's (;) main purpose is to signal a long pause or a change in thought, instead of a full stop that would be indicated by a period (.). It is often used instead of the word "and." For example: "You voted for him; I didn't; so what?" or, "I wrote last week; there has been no reply."

The colon (:) is a sort of signpost that points the way to the next thing you are going to say. For instance, "Here are three rules that you should follow: say it simply, say it fast, and shut up." Or, "There are three companies interested: Allied, General, and Imperial."

The comma (,) can easily be misused or overused. You can handle it without too much trouble if you bear one thing in mind. The comma denotes a short pause in a single train of thought. In action, a comma sets off items in a series: "We saw John, Joe, and Mary." A conditional sentence will also require a comma: "If I could, I would." Connective adverbs usually go between commas: "You, however, are mistaken." A comma will precede a person's identification: "John Rathbone, President of Allied Importers." A comma can lead into a quotation: She said, "Well, I think you could be right."

The question mark (?) hardly seems to need any explanation.

The exclamation point (!) I've heard very aptly called the astonisher. Example: "Wow! What an explosion!"

Parentheses ( ) and dashes (—) are all used pretty much for one purpose: to bring into a sentence additional or emphasizing material that is not *directly* connected with the sentence's topic. For example: "Sam Smith (our first president) started our company in that little one-room building." "That's the biggest—by far the biggest—generator available."

Quotation marks (" ") enclose what other people say. A single quotation mark (') encloses a quotation within a quotation. "She turned to me and said, 'I won't go.'"

The apostrophe (') has two main uses: (1) to make a noun possessive, for example, "The company's car," and (2) to indicate that you have omitted a letter or figure. Some examples are the contraction of cannot (can't) or "He is a member of the class of '48."

Punctuation marks are just little tools to help you clarify your sentences and make them easier to read.

Develop a Major Theme

The best business letter is one that is developed along one major theme. Once you have decided on your keynote idea, you must mentally visualize just how you will present it to the reader so that he or she will accept your proposal. The best way to do this is to place yourself in the reader's shoes. Ask yourself such questions as, "What's in it for me?" "What has the greatest appeal to me?" "Why should I do what he asks?"

Once you have decided on your major theme and the tone you will follow, and analyzed just what is necessary to sell the other person on your point of view, you must gather all data that will supplement your proposal. This information should prove your case, and it should be pertinent and not distracting. A person has only a limited amount of mental power available at any given moment, and the brain can only deal with one matter at a time.

There are other factors which also tend to confuse the reader. Try to avoid the use of complex or strange words, long paragraphs, and long, involved sentences.

The All-Important First Paragraph

You are now prepared to dictate or write your letter and your next step is to decide what you will say in that all-important first paragraph. Many executives claim that preparing a first paragraph that will attract attention is their most difficult and time-consuming job. Actually, the problem is minor if you have thought about what you want to say and have all the necessary data available.

In a good business letter, your first paragraph should accomplish the following two purposes:

1. Inform the reader of what the letter is about.
2. Make a favorable impression on the reader.

There is no reason why the recipient of your letter must scan through two or three paragraphs before finding out what your letter is about. It is also extremely important that a favorable impression be formed immediately. Your reader's attitude when reading the first few sentences will more than likely affect the reception of the rest of your letter.

You utilize the body of the letter to expand your main theme and also include all necessary data to help prove your points. The final paragraphs are important because here is where you tell your reader what you want him or her to do and urge action. You have already outlined your case and supported it with facts. In the last paragraphs, you must clearly state what these facts prove and what you expect your reader to do.

As with every human endeavor, "Practice makes perfect." This is also true of letter writing. If you follow the ideas and basic letter outline suggested, you will find that before too many weeks have passed, you will be producing polished letters. Of course, the final judgment of any letter will always be: Did it satisfactorily accomplish the purpose for which it was written?

Some busy executives I've met have developed form letters that are supposed to handle certain types of inquiries or complaints. This practice is acceptable to a limited degree. However, the form letter should always be carefully studied before being sent out. You can never tell when a few minutes spent writing a personal letter will pay off for you.

Writing the Right Memo

Just as letters serve as a communication link with the general public and business acquaintances, another form of communication transmits information within a company. This form is the memo, short for memorandum.

The use of the memo has skyrocketed in recent years. This rise can be attributed to the fact that in today's complex business world, oral communication is no longer capable of doing an efficient job. Executives and their subordinates today must assimilate and retain a multitude of facts. Because of the pressures of time and competition, it is easy to forget details. A written memo serves as both a reminder and a semipermanent record that certain directives were issued.

Properly used, memos act as important links between management and other personnel, and materially assist in the orderly guidance and control of a business organization.

Informational memos have gained wide acceptance in business today as morale builders. Management has realized that a lack of information about company actions or events can lower the efficiency and morale of the workers. Good workers have an interest in their company and like to know how events and happenings will affect them. Informational memos can be used to keep employees fully informed on all policy changes and other company news.

Basically the rules of memo writing are the same as for letter writing. You should state the purpose of your memo in your first paragraph. This is followed in the body of the memo by a detailed discussion supplemented by the necessary data. Your final paragraph will contain the recommendations and should point out how the reader and his company will benefit if the recommendations are carried out.

Preparing Reports

Reports are used today in a wide variety of ways. They can cover the activities of one person; analyze the operations of a department or a company for a definite period; disclose the financial condition of a firm; investigate a new product or market; report on an operational problem; or suggest a change.

Most reports can be classified into two main categories:

1. Reports that relate to specific phases of operations and contain only facts.
2. Reports that analyze and present conclusions and recommendations.

The first category consists mostly of routine reports and describes the gathering of facts and presents specific details without comment.

The more complex analytical report not only reports the facts but also contains conclusions and recommendations. This report usually contains a study of both past and present activities and may forecast future happenings.

I've found that most bad reports are bad because the writer did not have a clear idea of what was expected. Here, the fault lies with the writer for not seeking clarification of the assignment, and also with the individual who assigned the project.

Accepting the Assignment

What should you do if you receive the job of writing a report? The following checklist will help you get properly started. Incidentally, if you have the responsibility of assigning a report-writing project to another, just follow the same list when you pass out the assignment.

1. Make certain the project and content have been clearly defined.
2. Find out if the project can be limited to certain specific areas.

3. Find out if you are expected to make recommendations.
4. Get a completion date for the report.
5. Find out why the report is wanted and what its value will be when it is completed.
6. Be certain that you know exactly what is expected of you before you begin the project.

You should take copious notes and ask questions when the project is being explained to you. Only by doing this can you be assured of doing the job expected.

Requirements for Report Writers

Let's take a look at some of the requirements of a good report writer. He or she should be accurate, since important decisions may be made on the facts contained in his report.

Resourcefulness should certainly be a strong point. There is usually a hard core of information readily available to us on most topics. The man or woman who is resourceful makes use of this information, and then goes a step or two further to seek all new data and new sources to complete the report.

The last requirement is plenty of patience. The process of gathering and examining large amounts of data, as well as developing new sources of information, can be tedious. But if you are diligent and use your intelligence, your efforts will be rewarded with a good, solid presentation.

Language and Form

The final decision on how a report is to be written will depend on both the topic and the audience. If your report is being written for one person, it can be prepared in letter form. If the report is to be published or circulated to a number of people, it should be prepared in a more formal format.

The language you use will depend on the type of document. If an accountant, lawyer, engineer, or other specialist writes a report, it is permissible to use technical language only if the report is being read by others with the same background. If the report is directed at people without this background or to a wide audience, every effort should be made to cut the amount of professional terminology to a minimum.

Preparing the Outline

Assuming that you clearly understand your goal and that you have carefully assembled all the necessary data, your next step is to evaluate the material at hand. Examine all material for discrepancies and contradictions. Try to eliminate all data not directly relating to the problem at hand and summarize what remains.

Now, you should mentally review your material and visualize how it fits together. After you have done this, get your facts down on paper in the form of a written outline. This outline should contain an introduction, a main body, and a conclusion. This working outline should not be overloaded with details.

Writing the Report

Now you are ready to begin your writing assignment. Your introduction should state your purpose and the area covered by your report, as well as your sources of information. If your report is a lengthy one, it should include a summary of your findings and recommendations.

You should develop all the essential data for your report in a logical sequence. Long reports should have the subjects divided by certain topic areas. These can be subdivided if necessary. I strongly recommend that you use descriptive captions and subheads as reference points wherever possible.

After you have reported the results of your investigation and presented your supporting evidence, your final step is to present your conclusions. If you have been asked to make recommendations, do so at this point. These recommendations should be formally supported by the facts contained in the body of your report.

You should use exhibits whenever they will improve your presentation. Exhibits can include photographs, tables, graphs, and maps. They should only be used if they will clarify the facts that you present. Nonessential exhibits should be avoided if their only use is to beef up the report. These will only tend to confuse the reader and detract from the text.

As we mentioned before, short reports can be handled in letter form. Comprehensive reports should be arranged along the following basic lines:

Title page
Introduction
Table of contents
Body of report
Conclusion and recommendations
Exhibits
Bibliography

There is no easy way to write a business letter, memo, or report. However, you will find that writing is simpler if you follow the suggestions outlined and heed the rule that effective communications are *accurate* . . . are *planned in advance* . . . are *clear* . . . and are *brief.*

17
How to Prepare and Give Better Speeches

Men and women who normally make decisions that affect their very future without a second thought are often turned into quivering wrecks when asked to say a few words.

Whether it's a keynote speech at a convention, a few words at a club meeting, or a report to company officers, the idea of standing on their two feet and stating their ideas throws them completely. Such fear is brought about only by lack of proper training.

The fear of talking on your feet must be overcome because talking in public is not the out-of-the-way event it used to be for the average person. It is a sign of a person's growing stature when the number of invitations to speak in public increases.

Perseverance, Preparation, Practice

Three key words in becoming a good public speaker are perseverance, preparation, and practice. Public speaking requires that you be willing to work hard and devote time to learning how to do it. There are no simple short cuts to becoming a good speaker. Some people are born with the presence and the voice. If you were not one of the lucky ones, you can still acquire the skills.

You must be willing to spend time building your vocabulary. You must practice to develop a good speaking voice, and you must also try for orderly thinking. Whatever forcefulness or persuasiveness you are able to put into your speech will require careful preparation. And once your speech is written, you must work hard to perfect your presentation.

Your Obligation to the Audience

Any audience is important and you should remember that you have a definite obligation toward any group that has taken the time to come to hear you. Your speech must be both fitting and pertinent to the occasion. It should establish the fact that you feel your subject is important both to you and the audience. Never let your presentation drop below this level of interest. If you have thirty minutes allotted to you, give them thirty minutes of good, solid talk. Work hard to keep your pace high. You should think, speak, and act in terms of your audience's interests.

The first requirement of a speaker is that he or she have something to say. By this I do not mean that you can get up and say just anything. What you have to say must need saying.

As a speaker you must know the task that has been set for you by those who invited you, and just how far it is your duty to carry your audience. The question facing you is not primarily "*What* am I to say?" but rather, "Why am I to say *this*? What special knowledge or experience have I to pass along to those who are here to hear me?"

You may not want to sell a product or an idea, win a vote, or organize a committee; but unless you set a target for yourself, a desired reaction from your audience, your speech will lack vitality. And your audience will quickly know this.

Building the Speech

Like a house, every speech has to be built. First, you need a foundation, and then a framework to support the body of your presentation. If what you have to say tells the facts relating to a problem or a situation in such a way that your audience can easily follow your careful "construction," and if they feel at the end of your talk the way you want them to feel, then you have done a good job.

Preparation of a talk requires that you obtain current, up-to-date, and interesting information on your subject. You develop this information into a logical order as you build your talk to gain the purpose you had in mind. First you develop an outline. Your next step is to fill in the outline with the facts and illustrations you have found through research, and with your own documentation and proposals.

Every speech has three parts: the beginning, the middle, and the end. In having this characteristic, the preparation of a speech is not unlike the writing of reports or letters we covered in the last chapter.

You should plan to use your introduction to warm up your audience to the purpose of your address. The body of the talk will then be used to develop the facts upon which your thesis rests. The conclusion is the place to bring your audience around to accepting your point of view, and to acting as you want them to act.

Your first three minutes are vitally important. Unless you capture the attention of your audience during this time, you may not gain their complete interest at any time. Your opening sentences should be written to attract a favorable response, gain attention, and to lead into the rest of your talk.

Make your enthusiasm at being invited to talk to this audience very evident. Smile at them. If you have a good anecdote, use it. Try to show them you are one of "them." Get the audience on your side.

And one big warning: Don't ever apologize for being there. If you had nothing to offer, you would not have been invited. It is fine to appear modest, but don't beg off giving them a good talk. Remember—*you* are the expert.

The Body of the Speech

Once you've caught the attention of your audience, you must hold it. You must impress them, convince them, and motivate them to act. If you are making a report to stockholders, a safety talk to the scouts, a presentation to a service club or any other audience, take one hint. Don't try to turn them into a rampaging mob through the power of your rhetoric. *Do* attempt to increase their understanding and comprehension so that they will act in the way you wish them to act.

Your speech should continually move forward, carrying the audience toward the conclusion you want to make. You can do this only by carefully planning your talk before you give it. Point out your intense interest in your subject.

Vary your pace. If you normally speak at a slow rate, prepare occasional paragraphs made up of both short sentences and staccato words. If you are a fast talker, inject longer sentences to slow you down. If you fail to do this, you may lose your audience.

When you make a point, build it up and stick to it. Every time you digress, you weaken your story, and may even end up losing your audience.

The Conclusion

Just as your first few words are vitally important, so are the last few. Don't leave your audience up in the air. Make your ending an effective stop. Too many times a fine talk is followed by an inane, "I'm sorry for taking so much of your time." It is better to say just "Thank you" and sit down. Of course, the best conclusion is one which leaves the audience on the edge of their seats, just ready to act.

Preparing a good conclusion takes practice. But you will find it gets easier as time goes on.

Writing the Speech

Now that we've discussed the parts of the speech, let's delve into the actual writing. When you write a speech you should try to adhere to the following qualities: simplicity, good language, accuracy, and, of course, honesty.

Here are a few suggestions about what not to do. Don't write to display your vocabulary. If your audience doesn't know what you mean, you are certainly wasting their time as well as your own. As you write, keep asking yourself, "What does this mean?"

Your talk should contain simple, clear-cut ideas that will make your audience react to your proposals. Try to have one solid fact and an illustration to back up each main element in your talk. The facts may be from your own experience or from other sources. An important thing is to make your illustration appropriate.

How to Be Persuasive

Every speech should be persuasive. You should do more than merely describe the action you advocate. You should arouse the audience's desire to follow your suggestions. You can do this by expressing the proposed action with enthusiasm, and well-documented evidence.

The following outline will help you develop your presentation:

1. Show that a problem does exist.
2. Explain the essential elements of the problem.

3. Tell about any previous failures to solve the problem.
4. Describe your solution and the benefits it offers.
5. Show why your solution is the one best one.
6. Explain what you want the audience to do.

Sitting Down to Your Typewriter

I know people who can dictate or write a speech without any real effort. Few of us are that lucky. I know I have to work hard at it. The best way to start is to make notes as your thoughts on the subject come to you. Put these ideas down on paper at once so you won't forget them. I've found making an outline a real aid for the novice.

At this point you will find the following suggestions useful:

1. **Think out your subject.**
     Consider your audience and its previous knowledge and the best ways to reach them. How will your facts react on the audience?
2. **Consider your opening in which you pinpoint your purpose . . . your main body, in which you make your points in an orderly and progressive way . . . and your conclusion, in which you re-emphasize your important points and appeal for the desired action.**
3. **Consider all sides of the question so that you can answer any questions the audience may raise.**
4. **Write your speech.**
     Write as you normally talk, about 100 to 150 words per minute, and in the language you would ordinarily use in everyday conversation. See that your speech covers the time allotted for it, certainly no more.

Here are a lot of "do's" that will help give the "spit and polish" that a good speech needs.

Do use strong verbs.
Do repeat, but only for emphasis.

Do keep your sentences short.
Do use specific words.
Do write tight sentences when you need emphasis.
Do use the active voice whenever possible.
And some "don'ts" to be considered:
Don't use incongruous figures of speech.
Don't split infinitives.
Don't use highflown, poetic-type words.

5. Edit your speech.
6. Practice your speech against the clock. Trim it or expand it to meet your needs.

Before You Give Your Speech

Before you stand up, you should be fully prepared for the job ahead. Whether you are speaking from memory, from notes, or from a fully prepared manuscript—practice ahead of time. There is nothing worse than an unprepared speaker. The audience can spot it in seconds. Rehearse, rehearse some more, and then rehearse again.

Dress is also important. Don't let your clothes distract your audience. The loud Christmas tie from your mother-in-law belongs in a closet, not on display on your chest before an audience. Extremes in clothing should also be avoided. For men a simply patterned tie and a dark suit is best, although one well-known speaker on sales subjects uses a light grey suit and a bright red tie as his trademark. Your clothes should be designed to make you appear impressive.

If you are planning to speak from notes or a manuscript, make certain beforehand that the meeting committee provides a lectern. There is nothing worse than reading a speech with your head bowed to read the sheets lying on the table or held in your hands.

If you have visual aids, be certain the easel, camera, screen, or whatever is necessary is available before you are introduced. No interruptions, such as would occur if a chart fell down or if your slides didn't fit the projector, must be permitted to distract the audience from your presentation.

Your Introduction

While some masters of ceremonies like to prepare their own speeches of introduction, most are pleased to have the speaker give them a prepared one in advance. In this way you, the speaker, are assured of getting the type of introduction you want. Prepare a simple introduction and have copies mimeographed. Be safe: Even though you send an introduction ahead, carry an extra copy along in case the first one is lost.

On Using Notes

Whether you are planning to use notes or a manuscript, remember to place it on the lectern before you are introduced to the audience. If you have a title page, turn this over and have page one ready. The simple act of unfolding a manuscript or digging notes out of your pocket is distracting and may get your speech off to a bad start.

A word of caution: Make certain the people who speak before you or introduce you do not walk off with your manuscript. This is one very embarrassing way to lose your brains.

Now you are ready to begin. Thank the person who introduced you and make certain that you get the name correct. Thank the audience for having you and compliment them in some way.

Physically, you should appear natural and relaxed, but don't drape yourself over the lectern. You can rest your hands on the lectern, but only rest them there. I've known top executives who become so tensed up that their knuckles become white with the strain of holding on to the lectern and they look ready to tear the furniture apart. And stand steady on your own two feet; don't keep shifting around.

Smile, and Start Talking

When the introduction is over, smile and start talking. It is wise to talk a bit louder than the person who introduced you and certainly louder than your normal speaking voice. They came to hear you, didn't they? Keep your voice natural, however, and don't go in for old-fashioned flowery oratory.

A word to the wise: Watch good speakers perform. But don't try to imitate well-known TV or radio commentators. An amateur imitation very rarely comes off. The speakers you should watch and try to imitate are those who specialize in talking before such business groups as the Sales Executive Clubs. You might see if there is a local Toastmasters group and join for the experience and self-confidence you will gain.

Don't talk too fast. About 100 to 150 words per minute is just right. You can pace yourself by putting appropriate notes in your manuscript or by underlinings and markings in the margin.

Audience Contact

Don't make a clock or other inanimate item in the room, or even a single person, the object of your attention. Look the audience directly in its "face." Talk to one person and then to his or her neighbor. Swing your eyes across the entire group, stopping to talk to individuals in all sections of the audience. Appear to hold a conversation rather than give a lecture. Never turn your back to the audience. Communication on this personal level can put your audience in the palm of your hand.

While you are talking to your audience, watch for signs of restlessness. A yawn may call for more emphasis on your next point. Or it may be time for you to tell an anecdote.

Radiate energy, but don't pace back or forth—that will distract the group. There are also other things that will distract your audience, too: Don't pull at your glasses or your clothes. Don't scratch your head or body or smooth your hair. These are nervous habits that should be done away with.

Using Your Hands

Your hands are very important speaking tools. Don't anchor them to the lectern. Don't clasp them behind you or shove them into your pockets. Let them hang freely. Use them to make points, but don't flail them about. Use only gestures that come naturally. Don't light up a cigarette and begin to smoke.

Don't repeat one motion or gesture over and over. Watch the gestures used by trained speakers. Practice them in front of your mirror. You'll find that these motions will become very natural to you after some practice.

Grammar and Enunciation

Good grammar is important. But let me repeat what I said earlier, about the actual writing of the speech. Be sure you do not talk above your audience's head. There is no faster way to lose their interest. Speak in everyday terms and you'll be understood. It is also important that you do not appear to be talking down to them. Show that you respect their intelligence.

Good enunciation is very important and slowing down your rate of delivery will help you pronounce your words properly. If you make a mistake, don't go back and repeat the sentence. Chances are your audience forgot it as soon as you began your next chain of thought, if they even noticed it in the first place.

Watch the competiton. Stop if a waiter comes in. He'll get out much faster if he feels he has become the center of attraction. Don't pass out literature that goes with your talk as part of your presentation. You can have the materials already on the seats when the audience comes in, or get it to them after the speech is over. Actually, it is better to give the literature to them afterwards, because they are apt to start looking at the material in their hands as you start talking.

Using the Microphone

If a microphone is available, use it. Talk at your normal speaking level or a slight bit higher. Don't whisper into the mike. When the time comes to shout, step back a pace before you let loose. Don't hang onto the microphone and use it for support. If it is too high or too low, adjust it before you begin talking. Urge those in charge of the meeting to make certain that the microphone is working before the program actually begins.

Using a Manuscript

If you plan to talk directly from a manuscript, don't be ashamed and apologize for doing so. Remember all those famous politicians you've seen on television. They speak from prepared manuscripts, often flashed on a teleprompter the audience can't see. They do so because it helps keep them on the proper track.

Here are some suggestions that should help you to use a prepared manuscript. First of all, don't apologize to the audience for reading your speech. This is important. If you rehearse well before your appearance, chances are they never will realize that you are reading your talk. The rehearsal will help you deliver your prepared presentation at a normal speaking pace. It will also prevent you from lapsing into a dull monotone.

Practice tonal variations. Read as you would talk to another person. Dots, dashes, underlining, and capitalization will help guide your tone through the manuscript.

Your eyes should not remain glued to your manuscript. With sufficient practice, all you will need to do is glance at the first words of each sentence or the first sentence of each paragraph. Your eyes should bounce right back off the page and out to your audience. Maintain the personal eye contact mentioned earlier. Use gestures and take deliberate pauses.

A last word about working with a manuscript. Use a clean copy and make certain that the pages are in the proper order before you start.

The Anecdote

Many people find it difficult to tell an anecdote or a joke as part of their speech. They fear the audience will not find the story amusing and that the silence will be embarrassing. It takes practice to tell jokes. As a tip, tell only short stories. Very few people can tell a long humorous story to an audience. The funny stories or examples you use should fit right into your talk. They should not be told just because you feel it is necessary to tell one. They should be used only to illustrate points in your speech. And when you do tell a funny story, pause and let the audience enjoy it. Otherwise, the next portion of your talk will be lost in the laughter.

The more speeches you make, the better you will become. This is true if you practice and seek to improve. Go to hear well-known speakers. Watch their gestures, how they emphasize points, where they pause.

Your job is to arouse an emotional response in your audience. The combination of careful preparation and practiced presentation pays off. When properly used, the applause is more than politeness. It spells thanks.

18
How to Get People to Do What You Want

Several years ago I spent a day with two men, one of whom was considering the purchase of a franchised food shop; the other, a friend of his, already had one. The first man was trying to decide if he should invest his life savings in the business.

"Tell me," the would-be purchaser asked his friend, "is there one major point that is the secret of success in this business? Your place seems to run so smoothly."

His friend replied: "There is no secret. The answer is really very simple. It is just not easy to carry out."

"What is it?"

"Very simply, it's the ability to deal successfully with people. To practice what you could call good human relations."

Success is very often just that simple, whether you are your own boss or working for others. Whatever your job is or will be, there will always be people with whom you must work. Some people will have to be led. You'll have to work with others at the associate level. You'll also have to follow and work with any bosses who are over you.

This brings us to a very simple description of human relations. In plain language, it is the ability to get along with other people. It is also very much a part of this business of management we have been talking about. According to the American Management Association, "Management is the act of getting things done through people."

The Right Climate

Just how do we go about building good human relations? The best way is to build a climate or environment in which our associates will work with us, not against us.

There are two major keys to success in human relations. The first is to act and feel toward others as you want them to act and feel toward you. It is the Golden Rule. You may not think so, but your attitude toward others can be spotted by those who come to know you through working with you.

The second important key is your actual method of dealing with other people. When you know *how*, you can get others to do what you want.

Understanding Others

To be successful in human relationships, you must understand those with whom you are working. This is a very difficult task, because no two people are exactly alike. However, people do have certain needs, desires, and traits in common with other people. One fundamental requirement for effective leadership is a reasonable working understanding of what makes people respond. Once you have this knowledge, you will know what motivations can cause others to respond the way you want them to.

It's been said that all people have one or more of these four basic common denominators:

1. They want to be with other people and to be accepted by the group.
2. They tend to resist change. Habits form easily and most of us quickly become used to doing certain things in a certain way. If you want to change people's habits, you must do it in a gradual manner. This calls for patience.

3. Every man and woman wants to be important. It has been said that this is the strongest human urge. The key here is to try to see everything from the other person's point of view, as well as from your own.
4. Everyone wants security and peace of mind. You can provide this by making them confident, by letting them know that you feel they are doing a good job.

But People Are Different, Too

There is probably very little difference between two people. But even the slightest difference is the biggest thing in the world. People differ in one or more of these three things: the way they think, the way they feel, and the way they act. Let's spend a moment seeing why these differences do occur so that we can better understand others.

The way a person thinks depends upon intelligence, education, and ability to think logically. A man or a woman's feelings are regulated to a good degree by such things as aggressiveness, reactions to praise and criticism, and the so-called boiling point. Actions depend on thinking as well as physical strength and endurance, and coordination.

It takes practice in observation, and understanding on your part, to be able to determine the differences in people. This ability to analyze others will be a prize asset in helping you work with and handle other people.

How to Motivate Others

Now that we know the so-called common denominators in people, there are still other elements to be understood so that we can motivate others. Some of those with whom we work will be affected by only one or two of these elements;

others can be moved through the use and understanding of many.

Here are the things we should do to get things done by others:

1. A person wants fair pay.

> See that he or she receives it. This must be considered a primary consideration. Compensation ranks high on the list of things a person wants from a job.

2. Every person wants to feel important in the eyes of family, fellow workers, and the general community.

> You can give people recognition by praising them, by asking their advice, and by showing an interest in their working and, in some cases, personal lives.

3. Give every person a clear definition of what you expect of them.

> It is surprising how few people really understand just what is expected of them. One of the best first steps is to write out a job description for anybody working for you. In some cases, you should sit down with the man or woman in question and go over the job step by step.

4. Give every person an opportunity to advance and to grow within the organization.

> No one will work at top efficiency and give full loyalty feeling cut off from advancement.

5. Let everyone know just how well or poorly he or she is doing.

> You can best do this by setting standards of performance, by letting the man or woman know just how he or she is doing, and by giving help when it is needed. Every person has to know that he or she is an appreciated, partipating member of the team.

6. Job satisfaction becomes a good deal stronger if a person knows just how a superior will react in different conditions.

> If a leader is flighty and emotional and frequently shifts plans and policies, employees usually will be off-balance and confused.

7. Communication is important, and those working for a company will usually perform better if they know what is going on.

Several of our recent chapters were devoted to the importance and the techniques of communication. Certainly, one of the best ways to gain cooperation is to keep people informed so that they will know not only what is going on, but why it is happening.

Remember, also, that communication is a two-way proposition. It is also a flowback or feedback of ideas, suggestions, and opinions from those who work for and with you. Learn to be a good listener and try to evaluate what you are hearing from your people.

One of the best ways to keep the two-way street called communication open is to establish and maintain friendly relationships with others. Take advantage of every opportunity to talk to them. Such events as vacation selections, pay raises, and job instruction are good ways to start. You can create other opportunities by making it a habit to say hello when the employee returns from vacation or sickness, by meetings in the lunchrooms, by making calls when an employee is in the hospital or sick at home, and by showing a sympathetic interest in the other person's personal problems.

8. Delegate responsibility and authority to others, thus leaving you time to plan.

Try to have all decisions in your business made at the lowest possible level at which information is available. In this way you have freed your time for more important activities.

In delegating, it is wise to let your subordinates know that their whole future does not depend upon how well they handle this one job. Also assure them that you will keep in touch, giving them the opportunity to report both progress and problems.

9. When you must criticize, do it constructively and in private.

Get all the facts and review them with the person involved. Offer suggestions that will avoid similar errors in the future. A tip here: Before you criticize, see if you can give a bit of praise. Another suggestion, and a very important one: Reprimand in private.

One of my earliest bosses had a habit of publicly criticizing and crucifying his subordinates. I was just out of college, but I can still vividly remember top executives making five to ten times my salary mercilessly berated with the whole staff gathered around and the typing pool only a few feet away. It was no wonder that his people were afraid to come up with ideas and that the rate of turnover was always high.

10. **Praise and give credit where it is due.**

You can raise the morale and build the self-confidence of your people by giving them praise and recognition for a job well done. Another tip here: While you criticize in private, give your praise in public.

Remember, too, that giving subordinates credit pays off twice. Not only do they receive recognition, but you are given credit for building a good organization.

11. **Let your people work with you, not for you.**

Domination does nothing but breed "yes men". Those who do stay on with you quickly decide to leave their initiative at home.

12. **Don't give orders if you can make your wishes known by a suggestion or a request.**

People will generally produce far better work if they feel they are acting on their own than if they are ordered to do something. Then, too, they will do a better job if they know just why they have been asked to do something.

13. **Give your aides a feeling of participation by letting them in on the planning of your activities.**

This tends to make them more eager because they feel they are truly a part of what is going on. Another big advantage is that some of their ideas right off the firing line may prove a big aid in the finalization of your thinking. And don't forget that the opportunity to see how a program is developed helps broaden an assistant.

14. Show your people just what you expect of them by setting a good example.

This may mean that you will have to tighten up by making certain you are on time for appointments, that you do not take overly long, wasted lunch hours, that you don't take off to play golf when there is work to be done.

15. Show your people that you have confidence in them by asking for their advice.

This bringing them into the big picture is a big ego builder and also gets them to work even harder than they have.

When an aide comes up with an idea, he or she should be heard out, even if the idea seems useless. The objective is not to discourage them from thinking of ideas. The next idea may be the one that makes a million. If the one who has this idea fears to bring it forth, it will never see the light of day.

If you want to encourage others to think, plan, and to solve problems, tell them why their ideas are adopted, and also why the idea was bypassed. Only in this way can you help them develop.

When an idea is adopted, let its originator have the ball and run with it. He or she feels a personal responsibility for its development and will be a major asset to carrying out the idea.

Some executives have the ability to drop the seeds of an idea with a subordinate and let them develop it, thinking it is their own brainchild.

16. Plan carefully what you will say before you communicate it to others.

Carelessness in the choice of words, a frown or a laugh, a yawn, or a thoughtless shrug can all react to lower the morale and efficiency of those who work for you. Take care, because what you say may even cause the loss of good people. We discussed this in Chapter 13, but it is well worth repeating here.

17. **Let your people know in advance, if you can, of anything affecting them personally.**

This courtesy makes them doubly certain that they are part of the team. If changes are to be made, let them know why, so their own thinking and planning can coordinate with yours.

Cooperation at the High Levels

What we've just finished talking about is designed to help you get the cooperation and assistance of those people who work under you. Many of us also have the problem of improving coordination with others at our own level or a bit higher. Executives get better results when they know how to win the cooperation of others. This is vitally important. You can easily develop a raging set of ulcers if you run into a fight every time you want to do something.

Your ability to win the friendship and cooperation of others is an important success tool. You will have success if you have the patience, understanding, and skill to work along with others. Let's look at some of the guidelines to gaining cooperation from other people.

Perhaps first of all, be willing both to ask for cooperation and to give cooperation to others who need your help. In business there seem to be any number of people who will take assistance and then refuse to be of any help to others. There are even some who are so set and fixed in their ways that they cannot accept the help of others.

Second, be diplomatic in your dealings with other people or departments. Suppose the other department or person is causing mistakes, errors, or is lax. Your first impulse may be to accuse them of inefficiency. First count ten. They probably know they are having problems. It is needless to "expose" their weaknesses. All you may do is gain enemies, one or more persons who will oppose your suggestions. Probably the best way for you to handle it is to suggest that they may be operating under some very difficult conditions and that you do sympathize with them. Add that you have confidence in their ability to put your suggestions in action.

When you offer a plan, prepare your own schedule and stick to it. See that the others involved have their own time-tables so that they all can start immediately. It is often wise to arrange meetings so that progress can be checked. If problems seem to be popping up, see if top management will provide the extra help that is necessary to keep the program moving along on schedule.

It is often wise to have a coordinator appointed who is agreeable to all involved. It will be his or her job to see that everything is ready when needed. It may be unwise for you to assume the role of coordinator in some cases, because some of the others involved may object to your growing power. This is one of the problems facing an executive on the way up, and calls for diplomacy in handling all those with whom you are dealing.

Anticipate Objections

Never go into a meeting without having fully anticipated all possible objections and questions that may arise about your proposal. Sit down and note each possible objection and question and who might raise them. Then carefully plan your answers to each question. If you can anticipate which person will raise a particular question, you can develop your answer in each case to answer the objection. Diplomatic handling of the answer can often bring the other person to your side.

One thing to look out for is the older executive who may toss cold water on your proposal simply to see if you really believe in what you've said. If your proposal meets less than enthusiastic acceptance, don't appear completely disappointed and hurt. It is well to show that you can roll with the punches and come back with better ideas in the future.

What About Compromising?

Many business executives will be willing to try out a proposal, but in a limited way. If this is the case, don't reject a compromise. If your plan is good, a test will further support you. If there are any bugs in your suggestions, a small test is the best way to find what they are.

Your plan will probably stir up suggestions and ideas that may necessitate modifications. Accept them if they are good because all business growth has been a history of change and revision and compromise. If you feel that your plan is being emasculated and that the changes may cause it to fail, fight for your own ideas as hard as you can.

"Thank You" Is Vitally Important

If your proposal proves to be successful, don't take all the bows yourself. Let it be known that others were of great help. You will be able to count on their assistance in the future if they know they too benefit from your success. You can also bet that they will ask your advice and cooperation on their own projects in the future. This is the best way to get into the mainstream of operations within a company, a civic association, or any type of activity where you must live and work with others.

One quick tip here: When others have been of help to one of your projects, take the time to write them a note, thanking them for their assistance. It's a courtesy that is not soon forgotten. If people working for another executive have been helpful, write a note, calling this cooperation to the executive's attention and thanking him or her for permitting them to work with you.

The Skills of Leadership

The ability to get people to do what you want really means the quality of leadership you possess. The man or woman who is a true leader has the ability to arouse in others the desire to follow. You can improve your leadership abilities if you are willing to develop certain skills. Let's take a look at some of the skills that a leader must possess. Very few of us possess all of them.

Be a planner. One of the prime jobs of the manager is to organize. Leaders are always on top of every activity in which they are involved. They have the ability to see what must be done, and then to see that the necessary actions are carried out. They not only organize their own time, but also guide others so their time is most effectively utilized. And, as we have said so many other times in this book, they allow time to think about the future each and every day.

Make careful decisions. It is good common sense to weigh all facts carefully, to talk to all people involved, and to consider all alternatives before making a decision. This is just an extension of our discussion in Chapter 12.

Know and understand your people. It takes effort to understand just what motivates each and every one you work with and just why they act as they do. You must show a true interest in them and let them know you are interested.

Be able to communicate. An entire chapter, Chapter 15, was devoted to the importance of being able to communicate your wishes to others. All that need be said here is that you must possess the ability to explain what you want done so the other person clearly understands what is expected of him. There must be no misunderstanding.

Maintain performance standards. The ability to know and

understand the job requirements of every person working for or with you is a great asset to a leader. People become sure of what you expect from them and have confidence in their ability to produce, because they will know how they stand at all times. If you are familiar with the job description of your people, you will be better able to praise when praise should be given, to criticize when it is earned, and to provide aid and advice when they too are needed.

Ability to work with others. To obtain the cooperation of other people, you must be able to work with them without friction. This can be accomplished when your orders are eagerly accepted because others know why they are asked to do a job, and when the request has been made in a courteous manner. Your associates also appreciate it when you compliment them by asking their advice. As a result, they will go all out to assist you in reaching your goals.

Continually Practice Human Relations

The skills of good human relations can be learned just as you learn to play baseball or golf. They require that you be willing to work hard. Study yourself to find what skills need improving, and then make your plans to improve. After all, all we are talking about is another management problem— building a better executive. In this case, the finished product will be a better *you*.

The key to getting others to do what you want is to *practice* good human relations. There is a fifteen-word course in the subject. Its origin is unknown, but its meaning is certainly easy to understand and to use.

The *five* most important words are: "That was a good job."

The *four* most important words are: "What is your opinion?"

The *three* most important words are: "Will you please."

The *two* most important words are: "Thank you."

The *least* important word is "I."

19
How to Develop a Good Right Arm

A smart executive can find extra time by developing a top assistant. Choosing and developing a top assistant is a vital and important step for both the owner of a business and for a corporation executive. It is also a necessity for the president of the P.T.A. and any civic club.

Why is the development of an assistant so important? First, you add hours for other managerial duties because a good assistant can take part of your workload off your shoulders. He or she can do some of your management tasks while you concentrate on the important job of planning future growth.

Second, you develop a man or woman who can step into your shoes in case of an accident to you, an illness, or a needed vacation.

A good assistant may also be the means of continuing a small business if the owner dies and the family wants the enterprise to continue, even though they are not capable of running it themselves.

Choosing the Right Assistant

The first step in developing a top assistant is to make the decision to do so. Some executives have trouble here because it isn't easy for them to let go of responsibility. If the business is their own, any mistake the assistant may make is with their money.

Choosing the assistant is a major undertaking. If there is a relative involved, you may have little choice. But whether you choose from within your firm or family or from outside, how do you know you are getting the right person?

If the person is to be promoted from inside, you have had the opportunity of observing over a period of time. You can test him or her by giving management assignments prior to the promotion. If you get the assistant from outside, conduct a thorough interview. Check references and talk with former employers.

One important suggestion: Even though your assistant must have the same abilities as you do, try to find a person who complements you. Strangely enough, two dynamic and aggressive individuals are apt to set sparks flying in a short time. The capable assistant is usually one whose strengths match your weaknesses rather than one whose strong points match yours.

Qualities of an Assistant

You cannot expect to find a well-rounded manager who is ready and willing to move in to help you. You'll have to train and work with this person.

You need one who will profit from your experience. One who should be the type of person who wants to learn and can learn fast. One who should be able to think and should have common sense, with the ability to work with people and to gain their confidence. He or she has to be able to lead; becoming "you" to your employees and associates— and often to your customers and suppliers.

If the assistant has the qualities just mentioned as well as initiative, he or she can be taught to handle additional responsibility and authority; to learn the skills of management, such as planning, and the supervising of others.

You might, for example, assign your assistant the management task of hiring new employees. Learning such work will increase the understanding of the various phases of your business. The more he or she learns about it, the greater the satisfaction with the job. A good assistant will thrive on responsibility and a varied work routine.

How to Delegate Responsibility to an Assistant

In order to develop an assistant, you will have to work closely with the person. In addition to personal guidance, you should lay a solid foundation for your assistant's spot in your firm.

The following suggestions can be helpful here:

Give all the facts. See that your assistant has all the necessary facts about the new responsibility. Provide a clear picture of what has to be done and how he or she should do it. Tell how much responsibility he or she is to have. One way to start is by helping develop a description for the new job.

Tell the assistant who he or she will be working with and personally introduce him to these people. Make certain they understand that they are to deal with your assistant and not with you in the future.

Smooth the path. Inform employees who will work with your assistant that they must cooperate. You can smooth the path by spelling out for them the areas of responsibility you've given your assistant. Then impress on your assistant the importance of earning the respect of others even when he or she has to reprimand them.

Share your knowledge. Share your knowledge with your assistant. You must keep him informed of your plans, their progress, and your reason for making each move. Warn of problems that might arise. See that he or she learns the ins and outs of working with other people in your firm.

An executive who fails to give an assistant such background raises a handicap. By keeping the assistant partially in the dark, the executive sells the assistant and the job short in the eyes of those with whom he or she must work.

Add responsibility gradually. Give your assistant additional responsibility gradually to get the feel of the job. By being assigned additional responsibilities in small doses, he or she learns to handle new problems, thus continually absorbing additional knowledge and growing as a manager.

Hold a loose rein. Some make the mistake of trying to keep their fingers on every move that is made in their operations. Their constant checking may make their under- studies nervous and slow down their development. Rather than cause an assistant to lose confidence, and sometimes initiative, it is better to hold a loose rein.

Give him authority. Follow the management-by-exception principle when you give responsibility for a certain task. Provide the necessary authority to get the job done and ask that problems be brought to you only if something seems wrong or out of line.

Train your assistant to give you one or more suggested solutions to the problems brought to you. You then help the assistant develop by guiding him or her to make the correct decision.

How Much Control for You?

When you delegate authority and responsibility to an assis- tant, you are using another person's ability to think, to plan, to act, and to evaluate. Of course, you still have to keep control. Control is important so that you can blend their progress in with the overall activities of your business.

Check regularly on assignments which you give your as- sistant. However, as mentioned earlier, you will want to avoid the mistake of checking on each little detail.

A word of advice here: Your assistants probably will not do the job the way you would. Their approach may be as differ- ent from yours as their handwriting is different from yours. It may even be better. So long as they ethically get the results you want, do not nag about their methods.

Don't push your assistants onto the sidelines if you think something is going wrong. This practice tends to undermine confidence. It also lowers their status with the employees being supervised and with others with whom they must work.

What About Mistakes?

Everyone makes mistakes, and your assistant, without your experience and knowledge, will certainly make an occasional error. Keep in mind, though, that a smart person learns by making mistakes. Your task is to help him or her profit from them.

If you need to correct your assistant on a specific project, do it as we advised in Chapter 16—in private. On the other hand, always praise in public. In private, calmly discuss the mistake and point out how to avoid the error in the future. If you are too hard, your assistant may react by trying to cover up future mistakes. If this happens, you've lost communication with and have defeated the purpose of having an assistant.

Training an Assistant

The simplest way to train your assistant is to sit down and talk. You explain the day-to-day running of the business, the problems you face, the principles of management, and the plans and policies of your firm.

Then you turn your assistant loose, adding management responsibilities as fast as they can be assumed. Of course, you make yourself available to answer all questions.

Along with your discussions and his on-the-job practice in management, encourage your assistant to study and improve. He or she should read the trade publications in your line of business, as well as general business papers and magazines. He or she should also read articles and books on management subjects. One way to encourage such a program of self-development is by making the necessary books and magazines available.

Your assistant should also talk to suppliers' representatives and to customers in order to learn their views and needs. You can supplement this on-the-job training by using help from outside to orient your assistant. Some examples are:

Community and civic organizations. They provide a source of help, you might say, at your front door. When you encourage your assistant to participate in activities such as the Junior Chamber of Commerce, a civic club, or fund-raising drives, experience is gained in organizing projects. In these activities, he or she works without your guidance with citizens in your community. Many of them are your present or future customers.

Trade association conferences and conventions. A trade association is often a source of training help. Your assistant can attend a management institute if your trade association is one of those which holds them. Here your assistant will hear and learn from industry leaders and general business experts.

Many association convention programs devote part of their time to sessions on specific industry problems. In such meetings assistants can gain a better insight into the overall aspect of business. They can also make contacts with people of their own level from other firms. Such contacts can provide a source of new ideas and solutions to problems which firms similar to yours have overcome.

Supplier training programs. Some suppliers conduct management and sales training programs for business owners and their assistants. Sometimes such programs are conducted at the supplier's office or factory. In other cases, they may be held in the field.

Administrative management courses. Your assistant can study management at a nearby school or university. In some instances, these courses are set up with the cooperation of the United States Small Business Administration. Sometimes trade associations work in conjunction with the school. Usually, the instructors are a mixture of people from the school's staff and experts from the business world. I've had the opportunity to help organize such seminars and also to teach classes at many schools throughout the nation. Generally, they've been conducted at a really high level and are excellent training grounds.

Specific Training Techniques

Some of the techniques which your assistant may be exposed to in classes and conferences are: (1) in-basket training, (2) role playing, and (3) management games. Let's briefly look at each.

In-basket training. This is a technique used to teach men and women to make decisions quickly. Your assistant is given samples of paperwork that might reach the owner's desk. A decision has to be made on each letter, memo, or report. The instructor then evaluates these decisions and suggest improvements where necessary.

Role playing. In this method of training, the assistant plays the part of the boss and deals with problems which face the top man. For instance, the assistant may have to solve the problem of suppliers who can't meet delivery dates or customers who don't pay their bills on time. Other students act out the roles of the suppliers and the customers.

Management games. With this device, your assistant gets the opportunity to practice the art of making decisions. He or she is given facts of a certain management situation and asked to work out an answer. Then the decision is graded. Such games give the assistant an insight into the kind of difficult situations which can crop up in business management. They also show that often there are several possible solutions to such problems. The trick is to pick the most profitable solution.

Holding a Good Assistant

After you've developed a good assistant, your big job may be that of holding this person. Some business managers don't want to take the time to train an assistant. Instead, they let you do the job and then try to hire yours. You can overcome this possiblity by making it worthwhile for your assistant to stay and grow as your own job or company grows.

Right from the start, show your assistants that the job will pay off. Let them know what their prospects are for greater financial gain. You may want to outline your full plans for them. Or you may want to discuss only part of your expectations. If you withhold word of other rewards for various stages of development, make sure that they have an idea that you plan to reward their efforts as your firm grows.

In some smaller firms, the added responsibility that goes with being an assistant may bring the opportunity to buy part or all of the business in the future. I know one personable manufacturer's sales representative who was offered the second spot in a gas distributorship. Part of his pay was to be 10 percent of the business each year for five years. His employer planned to retire after five years and in this way he was making certain that his business would continue and that he would receive both income and profits from the business. At the death of the owner and his wife (they had no children), the entire business would become the assistant's. Here was a case where a man was able to buy a business with only his labor and brains.

Whether or not this is the case in your business, the good assistant deserves good wages and has to be paid well in salary or bonus. If an assistant isn't taken care of by one firm, often he or she will move on to another which does appreciate his or her abilities.

Developing a top assistant can pay off in many ways. It can make your own job easier, because an assistant can give you the time to plan for the future, and also to meet any emergencies that may arise.

With a competent and trusted assistant, you can take time away from your business to do things with your family. In effect, the proper assistant, after being adequately trained and guided, can help you to live a fuller life, both at work and at home.

20
Communicating Effectively Through Meetings I: Zeroing in on the Purpose

Sooner or later, you'll face the need to hold a meeting. It may be for employees, for staff members or executives, financing sources, or as part of your outside civic or religious activities.

At that time you'll find yourself as much in show business as any Broadway or Hollywood producer. The showbiz audience comes to be entertained. Your audience may be there because their jobs require it, or because they have a deep interest in what is going on. The producer's results are tallied at the box office. Your results are also measured. Someone, maybe you, must ask if your meeting resulted in more profits, or if other goals were achieved.

That brings us to the first question: Would your audience buy a ticket to your show? To get a "yes" answer, you must develop to the fullest degree your skills as both a meeting-planner and a leader.

Next question. And it is a vital one. You're going to call a meeting. Why?

"It's always been done on Monday morning (or every spring, or three times a year)."

"How else would I let them know about the new advertising program and schedule?"

"Top management always wants a pep talk at this time of the year."

"The new ad manger should get to know our people and discuss plans."

"I like to have each new supervisor get to know everybody during the first week."

Now weigh the cost of having a meeting for any of the above reasons. Even if it's only a small factory group, the cost adds up while they are away from their machines. And don't forget other groups or shops which become tied up.

If you're bringing salespeople or executives together, you have to take into account travel, lodging, meals, supervisory time, and planning time. It all adds up to a considerable amount of money. Often, a great many props must be designed for the meeting.

If it falls flat on its face, an even greater loss could be the respect of employees who see management stumbling around, wasting time.

In other words, if you don't have a good reason for calling it, chances are your meeting will fail. A word of advice: forget about holding a borderline meeting.

What is Your Purpose?

A successful meeting is rarely an accident. Planning and hard work are the secrets of its success. What I offer will work for business organizations and you can translate the information to your "after-hours" operations as well.

First ask yourself, "What do I want my meeting to accomplish?"

Try to write the purpose down in one or two sentences or paragraphs. If you can, you have accomplished several important things:

1. You have forced yourself to analyze your needs and you are better able to solve them.
2. You will know exactly what you want to accomplish.
3. You have set a goal of accomplishment for yourself.

The manager who does this regularly will produce a high percentage of successful meetings.

Why Hold Meetings At All?

Why are meetings held? The reasons vary according to type of organization, be it business, civic or religious. The prime motive, of course, is communication—and this is a two-way job. Management and employees, officers and members are on both the giving and receiving ends.

Basically every meeting is held for one or more of the following reasons:

1. To inform.
2. To train.
3. To inspire.
4. To gain feedback.

Let's look briefly at each.

Management informs employees when it tells them about overall market conditions, competition, management philosophy and goals, sales and production objectives, and changes in procedures. Officers of a civic or religious organization do a similar job.

Employees receive training when they are shown how to do something. If they are salespeople, a meeting may be designed to impart knowledge of sales techniques or specific information on selling one product or line. Plant or office workers may be introduced to new equipment or techniques. Management personnel may be kept up to date on new methods, voters on new civic issues or needs.

Inspirational meetings are used to fire up employees so they will do a better job. They may inspire people to get out and vote or to raise money for a church. It is at this type of meeting that management is put to the test of salesmanship. Management must sell its ideas to its workers.

Feedback is vitally important to management because it is an important means by which management can keep itself alert to employee thinking.

Information, training, inspiration, and feedback should be part of each meeting. If one or more elements are missing, success is harder to achieve. Here are several case histories to show you what we mean.

Case One

Objective. A department store wanted to increase the number of its credit card holders. Each employee was going to be urged to get customers, family, friends, and acquaintances to apply for a credit card by filling out application blanks the employee would give to them.

Information. Employees were told of the plan and of its importance to their employer. Each was given a number of credit card application blanks.

Training. Employees were not shown how to talk to prospective credit card holders.

Inspiration. Employees were told of the importance of gaining new accounts. They were offered a reward of $1 for each of the first five new accounts; $2 for each of the next five; and $3 for each additional account.

Feedback. Management did not ask if employees had any questions or suggestions. It did not follow-up to see why the program lagged.

And lag it did, because the average employee did not feel comfortable asking a person to take out a charge account at the store.

Now let's take a look at another, more successful program.

Case Two

Objective. To introduce the Wide Area Telephone System (WATS) to a white-collar organization.

Information. Employees were brought together in department meetings to learn about the new system and of the benefits it would bring to the entire organization.

Training. Telephone company representatives joined supervisors in going through the motions of showing employees how to use the system.

Inspiration. Employees were sold on the importance of the WATS line to their everyday business.

Feedback. Management and phone company representatives listened attentively to questions and to objections which were raised by those who could not see the need to wait for the WATS line. These were quickly answered. A follow-up was made after the line was in operation. Operators took note of employees having trouble with the line, and special training was scheduled.

This program was a success because all the elements of a meeting were included.

Preparation Is Important

Preparation for your meeting requires more than just knowing your objectives. Once you have carefully analyzed your reasons for holding a meeting, then you are ready for such other decisions as:

1. What is the subject of the meeting?
2. Who will be invited?
3. Where to hold the meeting?
4. How to best present the subject matter?
5. Who should make the presentations?
6. What program lineup or schedule should be followed?

Who should attend your meeting? There can be only one prime qualification. The only people to be invited are those who are directly concerned with the subject of the meeting. Having others sit in because "it would be helpful if they knew what is going on" can be a waste of time for both groups. Worse yet, it can lead to unnecessary interruptions and the buildup of adverse feelings among co-workers.

The best rule is to limit a meeting to only those who are directly affected by what goes on. Provide written reports to others, if necessary. Each of these is a vital point.

21

Communicating Effectively Through Meetings II: Developing the Plan and Program

An audience is usually sympathetic at the beginning of a meeting. Its members become excited participants or lapse into bored withdrawal only because of what happens during the presentation. Putting the program together, therefore, is a vital task for the meeting's organizer within management.

If your job includes meeting planning, you must first make time for your work. Those men and women who hold successful meetings usually do one thing: they plan continually. Every time they come across an idea or subject, they note it for future reference.

The easiest way is to set up a collection of file folders. These should be labeled according to the principal topics to be covered. After a while, as you add to these folders regularly, you not only have your next meeting organized but you have probably started on several coming ones.

These ideas will come from many sources. You'll find some as your read your newspapers, and general and business magazines. You'll gain other ideas through talking with people. Some ideas will be found by observing those who work for your company. Still more will be obtained at industry conventions and conferences.

Some organizations send a pre-meeting questionnaire to find out priority problems for possible discussion. Here's a questionnaire, designed to do just this:

As a participant in our meetings, you can help make our coming meeting most rewarding. Your cooperation in answering these questions will be helpful as we complete our program planning.

   1. Please list in order of importance five subjects that you think should be discussed at the meeting.
      1. _____
      2. _____
      3. _____
      4. _____
      5. _____

   2. A copy of the meeting plan based on the returns from this questionnaire will be sent to you before the meeting. At that time we ask that you tell us which subjects you want handled. Write a figure 1 after the topic you want discussed most. Write a figure 2 after the topic you think next in importance, and so on.

   3. Please give specific suggestions for our next meeting which you feel will make it more helpful to you.

It is not necessary to sign this questionnaire. Please return it by inter-office mail.

Working With Others

It is often wise to delegate some responsibility when planning meetings. This helps to assure you'll receive a fresh outlook concerning the planning of sessions, so that your meetings do not become stereotyped. The important point to remember is that the planner must set up an overall policy and decide how it can be best achieved.

There are certain things to consider once you have chosen the subjects for your meeting. You should know the following:

1. Which is the best type of grouping?
2. Who should present each subject?
3. How long should the meeting last?
4. Which is the best method of presentation for each subject?

Let's look at each, in turn, from a business organization's point of view.

Which Grouping Is Best?

There are seven primary types of groupings for those attending a meeting. You can use one or a combination.

Application Groups are used to try newly-learned information and skills in a practical situation. This technique works well with 10 or fewer people. Each group may have a mixed membership or may be composed of only those in one occupational line.

General Sessions are usually meetings of the entire organization. This is often the best way to provide information and to transact official business.

Occupational Groups are used if you aim your program at those in a particular classification. The size of these groups will vary, but smaller groupings usually work better.

Off-the-Record Groups allow participants to make suggestions or offer complaints. These are usually scheduled so that people will have a time to talk to their management during the program. As an example, one fleet leasing organization devotes the day before a sales meeting to having sales representatives meet in private with management.

Orientation Groups are used to start a meeting off. They help those attending to get better acquainted, as the participants are able to talk in smaller groups. The management conducting the meeting will use these sessions also to explain the timetable and everything else attendees should know, such as accommodations, meal and break schedules, rest room facilities, and transportation.

Special-Interest Groups are formed for those who are interested in specific subjects. The people in these groups exchange ideas, experiences, and opinions. The findings of these groups can be reported in general sessions.

Work Groups are often used to work out the answers to specific problems or to come up with recommendations for the organization. These groups may be composed of people with different job specifications so that a cross-pollination of ideas is obtained. Reports are usually prepared from the findings and suggestions of these groups.

Signing Up Your Cast

Who will star in your show? This depends upon your objectives, your organization, the type of meeting you will hold, and the subject to be covered.

Right here, we'll simply say that you should make every effort to have the person best qualified to handle each subject take part in your meeting. The stars may include you and other members of your organization, or speakers may be obtained from a variety of outside sources such as suppliers, industry figures, editors, or specialists in a variety of subjects.

Where and When to Hold Your Meeting?

Some meetings must be held on a company's premises because of their size or nature. Others will be conducted outside. The choice will depend upon the group and the subject.

This question is somewhat academic, because of the variety of reasons for holding meetings and the sizes and types of organizations.

Rarely would you take a group of factory workers away from their plant. The time wasted would make it foolish. If you were going to introduce a new procedure, you'd have to have the workers near their machines so that an actual demonstration could be made. In contrast, the introduction of a new model line to appliance salespeople does make a much greater impression if the meeting is held in a hotel ballroom, after a formal reception.

The timing of your meeting must be convenient for all who will attend. It should be a time that will cause the least interference with the operation of a company or one or more of its departments or divisions. The same is true for a state or national association. It is vitally important to survey all members of an association or executives of a company for help in choosing the best time.

For example, a major national association had been troubled by poor attendance at its annual meeting for a period of years. A survey showed that many members were hard at work preparing their budgets for the coming year at the time of the meeting. Advancing the date one month more than doubled attendance at the next meeting.

Travel time is also an important consideration. If people are coming in to a central location, they should be allowed sufficient time for arrival. Calling a meeting at 8 A.M. is a mistake if some of the attendees have a three- or four-hour drive. The alternative solution is the expense of having them arrive the night before. Some companies do this and hold a get-acquainted cocktail party. Such an event often makes it easier for people to get into the swing of the meeting. The ice is broken and people are more willing to talk.

Some firms prefer to hold their meetings over a weekend so that little time is lost away from the field or the machine. Rarely—unless the program or the meeting place is unusually attractive—do attendees appreciate this loss of their weekend. Their families are particularly unhappy about the arrangement.

How Long Should a Meeting Last?

No meeting should be any longer than absolutely necessary. The time needed will depend upon the subject and the type of meeting. Of key consideration are such things as time available, subjects to be covered, or objectives to be achieved, and the relative importance of each subject.

The longer a meeting, the greater the burden placed upon the planner's shoulders. To hold the interest of a group you must make certain your material is presented as interestingly as possible. The placement of subjects and speakers in the program lineup becomes especially important. The first speaker on the program, and at the start of each different session, should be a strong attention-getter. The closing talk should be of the same high caliber so that people leave all fired up. Weaker speakers or subjects should be sandwiched in between the strong segments of the program.

The meeting planner must also make full use of audio visuals and other visual aids, role playing, and other devices to keep attention keen. We'll cover presentation methods a bit later in this chapter.

Setting a Theme Is Important

During a recent election year, hundreds of meetings went off with all the excitement of a national political convention.

Banners, badges, music, and straw hats helped build up a motif that caught the audience up in the show. Experience has shown that a theme will help build enthusiasm and will help those who attend to recall what they hear and see.

The idea is to find a catchy theme for your meeting that will tie all segments of the meeting into one exciting package that puts over the company's objectives. Such a theme also helps give cohesiveness to a meeting. The theme can be set only after you've selected your objectives and then decided what subjects will be covered. It should be imaginative, as well, for the theme also has value as a means of stimulating the interest of those who have been invited to attend.

For example, one organization developed its meeting around the theme of a rocket flight through the solar system. Sales records would carry representatives from the earth to its surrounding planets. Arrival at each planet would put the staff at higher commission and prize levels. Advance publicity for the meeting was circulated using space illustrations and language.

One word of warning—a theme should be practical and should fit the conditions of the available facilities. A theme that is too difficult to execute or one that is trite or silly does little good.

Presentations: The Meat of Your Meeting

How should each subject be presented? The complexity of the subject will suggest the time for it and the techniques to be used in its presentation. Prolonging one session is as bad as compressing another into too short a period. Using just a speech to put over a highly complicated subject is also as bad as wasting visual aids on a simple introduction.

Some of the things to consider at this point are:

1. What are the goals of each presentation?
2. What is the best method for putting each subject over—a speech, a film, role playing?
3. Where does the presentation fit into the meeting-plan?
4. What is the composition of the audience?
5. Is there a logical order for presenting the different subjects?
6. Where should coffee breaks and lunch and dinner periods fit in?

Developing Your Schedule

A number of professionals with wide experience in planning meetings offer the following suggestions for developing a meeting program:

1. Allow breaks for questions at least every two hours.
2. Alternate different types of presentations to keep the audience on its toes.
> Don't schedule a series of talks one after another.
> Vary your program with a talk, a film, a skit.

3. Don't hold more than two or three presentations in a row without a break unless they run no longer than ten or fifteen minutes.
4. Your presentations should follow a logical order if at all possible.
5. Provide for coffee and soft drink breaks midway through your morning and afternoons.
6. Avoid having "heavy" subjects after heavy meals.
7. Present technical material in the morning or early afternoon.
8. Plan for recreation if your meeting is held away from company facilities.

This is better than letting attendees shift for themselves and possibly get into trouble.

Types of Presentations

There are five general types of presentation methods. Your choice will depend upon your subject, the audience, the meeting place, available time, and available funds.

1. The unassisted speech is the most frequently-used method of giving information.

It allows an "expert" to inspire the audience. The speech is less effective when used to present highly technical information or to give a variety of points of view.

2. The exhibit or visual type of presentation utilizes the leader as a commentator, using visual aids to present complex technical material, budgets, or reorganization information.

3. Situation presentations are demonstrations that illustrate "how-to".

Techniques include role playing, interviews, and skits.

4. Dramatic-action presentations are particularly effective in conflict or combat situations because they appeal to the emotions.

An example would be a showing of good and bad sales or telephone techniques. This method also works well when the group is asked to explore a problem. It is particularly effective when used for the final presentation in a session.

5. Panel-forum symposiums are used to present different points of view on a subject or to provide information on different aspects of one subject.

In many cases the leader acts as moderator. He or she asks the panel to speak and then summarizes its remarks. The leader also asks leading questions of

panel members and tries to bring the audience into
the act.

A Planning and Control Tool

As you develop your meeting, make it your business to map
out the program in advance. The best way is to set up a
timetable similar to the following one. With it you will know
who talks, at what time, using what method of presentation,
and requiring what presentation aids.

MEETING TITLE

DATES _____

TIME	SPEAKER	SUBJECT	PRESENTATION METHOD	EQUIPMENT NEEDED

Assigning Responsibility

A second (and just as important) part of planning is assigning responsibility for the makeup of the meeting. If you are not going to handle all planning, you should prepare a list of activities and note who will be responsible for each. For example:

Arranging and Planning Committee Meetings _____

Preparing the Agenda _____

Recruiting Speakers _____

Preparing Speakers _____

Supplementary Materials and Visual Aids _____

Direction of Rehearsals _____

Keeping the Meeting on Schedule _____

Entertaining Guest Speakers _____

Arranging for Meals and Refreshments _____

Arranging for Entertainment _____

Arranging for Reports of the Meeting _____

Measurement of Results _____

The above list can be expanded to meet the needs of any meeting. Just remember that nothing must be left to chance. Someone must be assigned responsibility for every part of your meeting.

YOUR
PERSONAL
LIFE

22

How To Gain
Self-Confidence

Lack of self-confidence is one of the main bars preventing many of us from living up to our fullest potential. It allows fear to take over and can limit us to only a small fraction of the success we could have in our business and personal lives.

Fortunately, you can increase your self-confidence. It will take time and effort, but once you have gained it, self-confidence cannot be quickly destroyed.

What Is Self-Confidence?

Perhaps the first thing we should understand is just what this factor called self-confidence is and how we can identify it.

Self-confidence is the inner conviction that you will be able to meet and overcome every demand that is made of you. A self-confident executive acts as if success is the only possible result of any and all projects undertaken.

This feeling will permit you to devote your fullest energies to meeting any challenge that occurs. There is no wasted effort or time spent in worrying about problems that will probably never actually arise. Ask yourself a question. How many men and women do you know who spend a good deal of time worrying about what *might* happen?

Two oil distributors serving a fast-growing suburban Midwestern area are prime examples of what self-confidence or the lack of it can do. Both knew they needed money to expand. Extra delivery trucks were needed, plant expansion was necessary. Their sales forces needed added manpower if they were to capitalize on the fast-growing market potential.

The first man was hesitant about approaching his local banker for help. He was afraid he wouldn't able to define his needs and plans clearly. He had always depended on outside accounting help and had never taken the time to learn to read his profit and loss statement and balance sheet. He felt insecure when it came to talking about money.

In contrast, his competitor had carefully planned for his own future expansion. He knew where his business had been, where it stood at the moment, and where it could go. He went in and presented a complete prospectus to the banker.

The banker quickly arranged for local and outside financing. Today, the second man operates a business four times the size it had been when he first sought monetary assistance. His insecure competitor had failed to even hold his own against increasing competition.

Self-confidence was the answer to one distributor's success.

A large LP-Gas distributor took the trouble to build a sound group of secondary managers for his decentralized organization. When an opportunity for a merger arose, he discussed the possibilities of the merger with these aides. They convinced him that he should discard the merger plans. Today, his organization continues to grow at an even faster pace than before.

When high transportation costs worried a beer distributor, he called his drivers into conference. He explained his problems and asked for their advice. Suggestions for reroutings, call reports, and preventive maintenance techniques and plans poured out from the drivers. He remodeled his entire distribution system on these suggestions. As a result, his delivery costs have dropped well below the national average for his industry.

The Effects of Self-Confidence

Self-confidence exerts a strong effect on your organization. If you believe in your own capacity to do the job, you generally believe in the ability of others to do the work assigned to them.

A confident boss helps build an organization because he or she builds better subordinates. He is able to delegate work and responsibility knowing that the work will be properly done and not having to worry about what is being done. This boss can ask and receive advice from interested, hard-working aides.

Building Self-Confidence

Self-confidence is built by successive successful experiences. You gain greater self-confidence through a series of successes in your business as well as your personal life.

The first step is to set goals for yourself. These could be personal goals such as learning how to dance, trying to stop arguing with your spouse, or taking the time to teach your child to play chess.

You can set such goals for yourself as a promotion, the success of an enterprise, improving your employee relations, or gaining a greater share of a particular market or clientele.

Setting Your Goals

Your goals should be long range. One thing particularly should be remembered here. In setting goals for the next one, five, or ten years for yourself and/or your business, remember that these goals must be reached in gradual but definite stages. This can be done by setting short-range goals to be reached in a month, six months, or one year. These shorter goals tend to act as guideposts or mileposts toward your final success. Every small success makes you feel so much more confident that you will achieve your major targets.

For instance, one oil distributor realized that he had only a small share of the potential volume gallonage that could be sold to industrial or commercial businesses. He was determined to gain a greater share of the market, and he wanted this gain by the end of the next year.

First, he surveyed the market to find the types and needs of local businesses. His next goal was to learn all he possibly could about the fuel requirements of these large prospects. Third, he readied a promotional and educational program to sell this new business.

When he had achieved his first goals, he was ready to step out after goal four, selling more gallonage to industrial and commercial prospects. His profits have risen greatly.

On Your Mark—Go!

Like the oil distributor, you have to set definite goals for yourself. Once these goals are spelled out, the big job is to get yourself moving. Getting started is in itself a hard job. Most people know their goal, but just don't know where and how to start toward it.

A proper start is often the most important ingredient in the success of any program. Actually making a start is simple if you will take the following five steps. They are simple and here they are:

1. Define the problem you must solve.
>   What must you do and what opportunities lie ahead
>   for you?

2. Analyze your alternatives and choose the one which offers the best opportunity for success.
3. Decide the best method to reach your goal.
4. Carefully recheck your plan and all other alternatives again to make certain you have made the wisest choice.
5. Get started. Act.

These five steps will help you overcome any indecision you may have based on any inability to organize yourself, as well as any lack of confidence in your ability to reach your goals.

How to Win the Confidence of Others

If you really want to bolster your confidence, be able to make others believe in you. When you have won the confidence of your associates, superiors, workers, customers, and the public, you have greatly built up your own ego.

There are recognized techniques that you can follow to build the confidence of others in you. Here are a few:

1. **Know your business.**
   Learn your business from top to bottom and become a recognized expert.
2. **Build others' confidence in you.**
   You can do this by becoming known as a person whose word is always good.
3. **Build a reputation for providing good work, service and value.**
   In this way, you gain recommendations for your business from others.
4. **Set high personal standards for your everyday life.**
   Follow the Golden Rule and treat everybody as you yourself would like to be treated.

First Impressions Are Important

First impressions are most important to help you gain the confidence of others. The four methods for getting others to believe in you just listed will help build your long-range reputation. There are also several ways to instill confidence at first sight.

1. Look and act prosperous. People find it easy to think you are on the ball if you look successful.
2. Look everyone straight in the eye. Many people believe this to be the sign of an honest person.
3. Be relaxed in the presence of others. This impression is catching and will help put others at their ease.

Sizing Up People

Another suggestion for building your self-confidence: Learn how to size up other people quickly and accurately. This is essential. When you can size up other people, you will feel more self-confident because you will be better able to sell or influence the people with whom you are dealing.

There are definite guides to help you size up the people with whom you'll come in contact:

1. Know what you need to know about every person that you will meet.
2. Study the person closely—clothes, office, home, friends, interests, mannerisms, and actions.
3. Listen to the other person. See if his or her ideas are well organized. Are they presented intelligently? One of the best ways to study another person is to draw him or her out by skillful questioning.
4. Ask others about the people in whom you are interested.

The Tools for Your Success

To reach your goals you are going to have to make the fullest use of all your abilities and training. And this book will help.

Read and then review the material in this book to help you improve yourself. For example, Chapter 12, "Thinking Your Way to the Right Decision," will help you decide on your primary needs and goals and how to go about achieving them. Since progress demands study, Chapters 2, 4, 5, and 6 on faster reading, learning, time management and cutting deskwork will give you the time necessary for improving your knowledge.

Because the self-confident person must be able to work at the fullest capacity, Chapters 7 and 8 on staying healthy and working under tension will prove extremely helpful. Chapters 15, 16, and 17 on better writing, speech preparation and presentation, and overall communication will help you put yourself over to others. The important ability to profit from your mistakes is also worth reviewing in Chapter 13.

Self-confidence is often the difference between major and minor successes, and even between success and failure. Your growth in business and in your personal life is so important that you must make an all-out attempt to build a more confident you.

23
Your Community and You

People—we are born in a world full of them.
People—we have to live with them.
People—we depend on them for our living.

    A community is not just homes, streets, parks, schools, churches, buildings, offices, and places of business. A community is also *people. People* are your prospects. Prospects become your customers. *People* work with and for you.
    These *people* are the public. Their reaction to you in your relationships with them—good or bad—must be good or bad public relations.
    How, then, can you better know the people of your community and, most important, have them become favorably aware of you and your business?

New Place for Businesspeople

The day is gone forever, when business executives can limit their interests only to their own business. Today, the public expects them to take the lead in building a better community.
    Some cities are growing richer because leading businesspeople are taking the time to help build a better community. They help redesign city charters, clear slums, modernize old

sections, attract new industry, promote better schools and cultural centers.

A decaying community would be the wrong place to start and build a thriving business. It is becoming increasingly hard to operate a successful business, even in the better parts of any community, unless there is an awakened public doing something about any slum areas in the whole community. The slums tend to strangle the progress of the entire area surrounding them.

Community Relations Guide

Building good relations is more than just meeting a customer with a smile and seeing that he or she is satisfied with your products and services.

You must seek out ways to make friends with customers, employees, financial sources, suppliers, and the general community. This can be accomplished by taking part in community activities, contributing to charities, working with associations and attending conventions, and even planning so that your retirement will be beneficial to the community, as well as yourself.

Community activity has become so important that the old excuse that we cannot afford the time it takes is dead. We cannot afford *not* to take the time such activities require.

Civic Affairs Participation

The executive taking part in civic affairs learns of things which are being planned in the community. You find yourself associated with people who virtually control the present and future prosperity of the community in which your business is located and the future of your community has a very direct effect on the future of your business.

Take a look around your town. Make a list of the 10 most successful business and professional people who live there. Look at them as citizens in your community. In most cases you will find that they have either been, or still are, very active in those things that contribute to the good of the community.

There is a well-established relationship between these civic activities and the success of a business. However, you will find that most of these people do not enter these activities for a purely selfish reason.

The sincere, public-minded person is a dedicated person who is the first one to be pleasantly surprised at the rich dividends and benefits received through good works. The one who begins this work looking only for the rewards soon is left out.

Moving Ahead in Organizations

We must emphasize that it is of absolutely no value to be only a joiner. It is positively necessary that you take an active part in the committee work of an organization.

As a member of any organization, it is necessary to make yourself known to its membership without becoming a "glad-hander" and a nuisance. You must know who they are. They, in turn, must know who you are.

It is not enough to arrive promptly when the meeting starts, only to run away at the close. The five or 10 minutes spent before and after the meeting is time well invested. They permit members to get to know you and identify you with your business, while you get to know them and their business connections.

One rule is important. Contribute something to the meeting or get out and into some other work in which you can make a contribution.

Local federated fund drives are easy ways to expand your circle of acquaintances. Through your participation in these drives—whether United Fund or Community Chest—you meet your neighbors in the homes or places of business. You find yourself closely associated with people of good will and ability in your area.

Ready-Made Groups for You

The small business executive or owner can belong to the small community area booster club, the Junior or Senior Chamber of Commerce, or whatever name might be used for these local organizations. There are many other chances to serve. The Cub Scouts, Boy Scouts, Boys Clubs, Little League baseball groups, are only a few of the possibilities. The parents of these youngsters generally feel indebted to the one who takes time with their child. Throughout the year you keep meeting family units. Each year brings with it new groups.

Managing Your Time

You must also fully recognize that in all such organizations there are innumerable jobs to be given to a person who does not properly study the contribution he or she could and should make in the community.

You can become so loaded with assignments and involved in so many activities that you will find you are neglecting your own business, even to the point of failure. It is more important to do a few things very well than attempt to be all things to all people and fail miserably in the effort.

A well-developed sense of timing must be used to be sure that community jobs are done and done well. Future jobs must be planned so that you and your business are kept before the public periodically in a favorable manner over an extended number of years.

When this is done, everyone wonders how you found time to do all of these things and still operate a successful business. Again, if you check the 10 most successful business-people in your town, you'll find they did one thing at a time and did it well. They spaced their contributions so as to be able to do well that which was for the good of the community. At the same time, it paid off for their own business.

The more careful your planning, the more in demand you are. You are placed in the position of being sought after by top community businesspeople for advice. You can graciously decline many more jobs than you ever undertake. You can choose the ones for which you have time and are best suited to handle successfully.

Appreciate Assistance

In your work outside your business, as well as in your own operations, you should develop a high and sincere sense of appreciation. A good employee can become indifferent. A friendly citizen can become resentful for not being properly thanked for a job well done.

While we must always keep our feet planted on the firm realistic rock of sound business practice in our everyday life, we must never lose sight of the fact that to grow tall and to be successful in our business or community, we must work at possessing idealism and ethics.

Employees Part of Team

In your business, be it large or small, recognition must be given to the fact that where the public is concerned, every one of your employees actually represents your business. Many well-written books are available on the importance of the properly trained telephone operator, secretary, clerk, driver, or service station attendant. Each of these people plays an important part every day in creating a feeling of friendliness and goodwill for the business they represent.

Recognition of this situation points up the need for improving communications between those running the business and their employees. An employee cannot possibly tell the public the good things about a company and its products and services unless he or she is fully aware of them.

A feeling of belonging is tremendously important to every employee if the company wants to have good public relations and to prosper.

Community Development Leaders

Today's economic and legislative forces have opened a major vacuum in community leadership. It is to your interest to step in and take hold. As your business grows you'll have more time and money to devote to public work.

Those who realize this structure their organization so that they will have the time to become community leaders. Here are some of the jobs awaiting you when you become a worker for your community:

1. Get into politics—try to balance income and public expenses.
2. Build community credit by cultivating the municipal bond buyers.
3. Train people to restrain expenditures which will not pay.
4. Make the community more attractive and pleasing.
5. Encourage all who meet strangers to be hospitable, gracious and helpful.
6. Educate the young to be business-minded.
7. Teach business management how to raise capital.

8. Fight to end slums and other community blight.
9. Make the community a more hospitable place for new business.
10. Lead charitable drives.

The Public Relations Job

Regardless of the size of your company, you as an interested person are the best public relations officer your business has. No staff of experts can do more good or more harm for your company than you.

A great majority of our most successful politicians or statesmen give proof of the value of good public relations. They belonged to small civic groups at first. They became active in local politics. They became identified with those things which were good for the community in which they lived.

They realized that their existence and continuing success depended not only on being favorably known, but also on knowing people who would be willing to contribute to their campaigns and work as volunteers to keep them in office.

You Can Do It

We all like to act and feel self-sufficient. That is the way we are supposed to appear in public. Most of us, however, worry about our abilities. We hide behind shyness and self-doubt. We turn down requests for our help on the grounds that we are not cut out for that type of work, that we cannot afford the time it takes.

Almost without exception, the leaders in every community were discovered among those who began to discharge their community obligations by serving modestly, even re-t2on22222222222222222222222222222

luctantly. The community discovers a new leader who begins growing more successful all the time.

If you will undertake your responsibilities to your community, if you wisely invest your time and talent for the benefit of your neighbors so they will come to know you and like you, they will express their appreciation by giving you their business and influencing others to visit you. As your community prospers, your business and personal prosperity will parallel the growth of your community.

24
Are Your Ethics Showing?

One of the biggest problems facing a business manager is that of ethics. Does your community trust you? Your future, that of every business, and even our free enterprise system depend on public trust. Social responsibility is one of your biggest management jobs.

Our society's prosperity is based on business success. Therefore, the reputation of our business leaders is pretty vital to future survival. To be truly a leader in your community, you must have its respect.

Keeping Your Reputation

People are basically honest. Sometimes, however, the pressures of competition force them to act in a way which goes against their consciences. Once this happens, trouble begins brewing. If a reputation is ruined, a business may fail. Fine names built up over many years vanish in an amazingly short time.

A whole body of traditions, laws, and ordinances have grown up over the centuries that directly affect your business actions. We are in an era when private business is to be judged in terms of its contribution to the general welfare.

Ethics have a definite place in our business life. Very simply, ethics mean selling good products or giving the best service. Ethical people avoid the use of shady practices such as bribery, false attacks on competitors, short weight, or improper or incorrect claims in selling and advertising. They maintain legally required conditions of safety and sanitation, observe regulations, and are honest in all their contacts with others.

Effect of Your Actions

By building a stronger and more profitable business you have set certain goals for yourself. These goals are all important to you, yet you have a social responsibility toward your community to see that it is not hurt. With each goal you must ask yourself certain questions that pertain to your community. How will your actions affect your employees and the many people who depend upon them? Will plant location changes or general operations lower the value of neighboring areas? These are only a few of the many possible questions arising.

The moral problem you face is to realize the social effects of your decisions and to consider how far you can move toward your goal by modification of your decisions.

Winning Prestige

If your community progresses because of your activities, you gain prestige. You are looked up to as a business leader. You are asked to lead charity drives, slum clearance, and cultural projects. This prestige cannot be bought by money. It is only won by hard work.

One touch of scandal will wipe out a good name built over generations. You just cannot afford to be unethical.

Some use the excuse that they must resort to sharp practices because of competition. This varies from such unethical practices mentioned earlier as kickbacks all the way to short weight. It sometimes includes practices which are not basically illegal. This would include ridiculous pricing that destroys profit for all. Or it might be the telling of lies.

Setting Industry Codes

Your reputation does not only depend upon your own actions. The activities of other business people reflect upon you. Shady practices exist in almost every business. Doctors have been accused of directing patients unnecessarily to specialists to gain by fee splitting. Some businesses display a permanent "going out of business" sign. Repair and service people of all types have been under a cloud of suspicion by unknowledgeable customers. In perhaps 99 percent of the cases, this is not true.

One merchant sold his Cadillac and took to driving an old beat-up smaller car. His clothes became seedy. A month after these carefully planned actions he cleaned the floor of appliances with a "Need Money" sale. A week later the well-dressed businessman was back driving a brand new expensive car. He had successfully acted out a part.

Many businessmen have banded together to clean up their industries. Sometimes their "codes" have been too "ivory-towerish." Generally, they have achieved major success in one direction. These attempts have brought together men and women with mutual interests. Associations and even promotion groups are good examples. You and your competitors have learned to exchange views on business conduct and practice. As a result, your mutual understanding is stronger.

Some years ago a magazine of national reputation boldly attacked both fuel oil and LP-Gas distributors, among other business owners, for short-weighing customers. LP-Gas customers were cautioned against allowing deliverymen to make a drop with a second line attached. The article's authors were completely ignorant of the importance of this vapor return hose.

A fuel oil scandal in an eastern city caused the public to worry about all metered fuel oil deliveries. This was the action of a few scattered dealers.

The public is too ready to believe a business owner guilty. You must maintain the highest ethics at all times. In this way your reputation will not only stay clean . . . it and your business will grow.

Employees' Ethics Important

Ethical actions by your employees are also important. A salesman who misrepresents quality or terms . . . the occasional deliveryman who steals and tries to cover by shorting other customers . . . the employee who steals from the register . . . these people can ruin your business reputation. Careful selection, proper pay rates, adequate supervision, and the ability to instill pride in the job will help you build a better employee.

There may also be the case of the employee who is forced by a boss to be dishonest. Your job as a manager is to get employees to work to the fullest of their abilities. It is much easier to bring employees to this goal when they feel good about what they are doing.

To ask a worker to do things that make him or her feel guilty is bad. He or she will do a poor job. Encouraging ethical actions also keeps them on the job longer. Many employees quit because they don't want to be dishonest.

Dealing With Customers

Your employees' contacts with the public are extremely important. They should follow certain rules in dealing with your customers. These rules will insure the continuation of your good name.

1. Sales people should thoroughly understand your contracts.
2. They should make certain that customers read and fully understand all phases of the contract.

3. Sales people should know your policies about contract enforcement, adjustments, payments and repossessions.
4. Sales people should avoid outright misrepresentation of facts.
5. Sales people must know company policies and the bounds limiting their own authority to commit the company to any action or responsibility.

Relations With Employees

Ethical business relationships with your employees are another important part of good operations. The workers who are dissatisfied will pass these feelings along to your customers and the general public. Their family and friends also become sounding boards for their bad feelings. The circle of contacts of these people is even greater than that of the individual worker.

If an employee is wrong, you, as the boss, must correct him or her. This is one responsibility you cannot avoid. Many times hard feelings happen because of misunderstandings. Make certain that all policies and commission and pay plans are fully understood by all before they are put into effect.

You also have the added responsibility of protecting the life and limbs and health of your employees as well as the general public.

Outside Activities

It is to your company's advantage to encourage your employees to take part in civic activities. They gain valuable experience in leadership, planning and administration when they hold key posts in church, civic, fraternal or professional groups.

Not only do these activities aid in the developing and maturing of your employees, they continually place your company's name in the public's eye as a leader in building a better community.

Your own outside activities also play a big part in the picture you have developed of yourself. Chapter 23 focused in on this role. If you take the lead in outside work, you must keep your skirts clean of any taint. One slip will put a black mark against your company, even if it is not involved.

The Problem of Bribes

In recent years, closer controls are being put on businesses of all types of different branches of the government. Some executives have taken to bribing inspectors or purchasing agents and even government, here and abroad. These actions are certainly not ethical. The business executives blackmailed into a bribe to continue to do business in a way that is against the law are open to similar actions throughout their career.

A Continuing Problem

Ethics and business responsibility are continuing personal problems. Each of you must decide upon your own code of morality.

If the ethical problems arise at any given time, take a few minutes to ask yourself some questions. Is what you are doing fair? Is it reasonable? Is it just?

Your rewards are simple to define. *They are the three "P's"* . . . *Pride, Prestige and Profit*: Pride in being a clean business leader. Prestige gained among your customers, the general community and your competitors. And last, but certainly not least, ethical actions bring both profit and success.

25
Planning for a Happy Retirement

It is generally agreed by students of retirement that the four ingredients of a contented life in retirement are:

1. Financial security
2. Good health
3. A happy home life
4. A purpose in life

These four ingredients are usually discussed in the order given. But they may well be better considered in the reverse order. It is wonderful to have enough money to do anything you want, but it is a complete waste of effort to accumulate this money and not know how to put it to the best use.

Money and Purpose

If you are a success in business, you are taking a big step toward financial security. You have learned the value of the dollar and the need for saving and financial planning. So, too, the getting and keeping of good health and a happy home life are "how-to's" of acquiring a happy retirement.

In the fourth ingredient—purpose—you not only have a "how" but the *why* of planning for retirement. You have the answer to the important question: "Why should I be so concerned now with the years after I retire?"

Thinking about retirement now is important because old age can come upon you gracefully—or disastrously. How old age finds you is pretty much of your own making. Just how well you approach your old age depends upon how well you grow up physically, mentally in your general interests, and emotionally. Your attitude toward these four parts of the aging process can speed up or slow down the speed with which you grow old.

Some people reach old age intellectually the day they leave school. You've heard of people referred to as old before their time. They make no effort to solve any more problems. They are not interested in exploring new subjects or ideas. They are content to confine their reading to popular magazines, to newspaper sports pages, and to escapist literature. Some with even less interest in life become wedded to their television sets.

Yet others stay curious about the things that go on around them. Can you think of a more exciting time to live than today? People with a purpose seek to keep up with these fascinating times. Those of us born since the turn of the century have seen almost as much progress as has happened in all the years since the earth came into being. The alert ones try their hands at studying new areas of science, or a foreign language, or enroll in some study or hobby class. This type of person can, and often does, stay intellectually alive and young at 60 and 70 and 80. One of my friends took up the organ at 60 and became a really fine player. Another retired to a very active role in politics. He put his managerial abilities and experience to work doing some very vital work in helping his community reorganize much of its town government.

Check Your Social Habits

The years before you retire are the time to check over your social habits and to prepare yourself for the days in which all you'll have to do, perhaps, is mingle with people on a social basis. This analysis is vital because if you tend to avoid people at 30, or 40, or 50, you may be a hermit at 60. On the other hand, if you make it a practice to seek people out in those early years, you'll not run short of friends later in life.

Remember also that you can't be a worrier or a hater during your youth and expect to find peace of mind at 65. A person continually complaining about his minor aches and pains, trying to live in the reflection of past glories; who talks too much, or shows over-anxiety, is often showing signs of emotional deterioration and approaching senility. It is important that you keep zip in your thinking as well as in your step.

If this seems to be a lengthy introduction to the actual planning for your retirement, it is done for a reason. It is necessary to understand why some dread the thought of retirement, while so many of their co-workers look on it as a welcome opportunity to catch up on their hobbies, with reading, a chance to travel, and, most importantly, a time for greater companionship with their spouses.

People who fear retirement may see themselves facing a period of aimless puttering while they wait to shake hands with death. These are the people who will actually devote very little time and preparation to retirement. They use all sorts of excuses for not facing up to retirement. They may see, or pretend to see, little chance that they will be able to afford retirement. If sickness or injury forces retirement, they are mentally and emotionally unprepared for it.

Plan Long in Advance

The person who is growing old in a healthy manner will make retirement plans long in advance. This is important. Perhaps you feel that you would rather enjoy life now than make sacrifices for an event that may seem very far off. If this is so, it is wise to consider that advance plans do not always include sacrifices.

Too often, it is the person who failed to plan ahead who must sacrifice. Many husbands and wives who have been used to country club living suddenly find that their house, their car, their friends, and their very way of life are just too expensive for them once they retire. Careful planning and investment could have assured them a comfortable standard of living.

To go a bit afield in this talk about planning: Have you ever waited too long to make a hotel reservation and found that when you got around to it there was no room? Or have you had the experience of planning a trip, a visit, or an evening out, and found that you had as much fun anticipating the event as you did at the show or on the trip?

The point being made here is that to enjoy life at any age, not just at retirement, reasonable thought and planning are needed. People who depend too much on luck seldom get what they hope for.

Assuring Your Future Security

Security in retirement is not a product which someone can manufacture and hand over to you at age 65 along with your retirement gift of a gold watch. Security is the fruit of years of growth, of developing your attitudes and emotions, of making personal plans.

A mature person feels secure being able to handle the responsibilities of everyday business life. So older people need to feel secure by reason of their own activities.

The Greatest Danger

The greatest danger to you in retirement is the loss of purpose or the reason to live. By the time most of us have reached 40, we have come to realize the importance of work in our everyday lives. Even after we retire, we must keep usefully active in order to feel that we still have a place in the scheme of things. If you acquire the feeling that nobody needs you after you have retired, you will doubtless find your old age a burden rather than a pleasure.

The idea of being able to take it easy will probably sound very enticing in your pre-retirement years. But if taking it easy merely means a routine of eating, sleeping, reading, and watching television, then you are likely to find that you are drifting into a state of unhappy idleness. Most of us need some stimulating activity to give our lives direction and purpose.

One friend retired not so long ago after 50 years "in harness." For two long years he had looked forward to the day of his retirement "when he could take things easy" and realize a life-long ambition to "travel and see." Six weeks and 10,000 miles later he was back home, with the flat statement that he had enough of driving and sightseeing. Today, this same fellow is performing the duties of acting treasurer for his church and taking pride in his new-found responsibilities.

Look for Variety

One of the important things to remember in planning for activity after your retirement is to leave a couple of doors open. The pot at the end of the rainbow that looked so good at a distance may not stand inspection at close range.

Some people in business are in a position to gradually reduce their workload as they grow older. They may, therefore, need no plan for useful activity in their old age. But others are called on to retire from full-time jobs all at once. The answer is to be ready with carefully laid out plans for doing something else when the last day on the job comes.

You may want to try your hand at operating another type of business, such as one that may be developed out of a hobby. Some businessmen with knowledge of some phase of management have founded new careers as consultants. In 1964, the Small Business Administration organized a group of volunteers who aided small business owners. This is called the Service Corps of Retired Executives (SCORE) program.

To be as successful in the retirement business as you are in your present occupation, you should carefully study all the possibilities and thoroughly plan your moves in advance.

Work Today for Tomorrow

From the standpoint of peace of mind, any activity that is not dangerous to your health is useful. There are, however, certain activities which can bring even greater rewards in self-respect and the feeling of accomplishment. The key thought here is that these activities must be engaged in before you retire so that you can set the groundwork for your after-retirement participation.

Some of the examples mentioned in this chapter show how people have successfully taken on interesting activities in such areas as civic affairs, church affairs, and politics. But they had either been involved somewhat before, or knew someone influential in the group.

The person who thinks that all he or she needs to do on retirement is to show an interest in civic affairs is likely to run into a stone wall of indifference. Unless you have an "in," few groups will be interested.

There is evidence that the person growing older is more apt to give greater attention to spiritual matters than in early life. Yet, if you have rarely stepped into a church before retirement, you are not apt to find much comfort in church activities after retirement.

You may not even write that book you always planned after retirement unless you have been doing some writing before retirement. Many people feel they have a great story or two to tell. Yet, once they retire and have the time, they just don't know how to sit down in front of a typewriter and begin.

In short, you are not likely to do any of the things that look attractive to you as post-retirement activities unless you have done some of them before you stopped going to work on a regular basis.

Determine Your Values

Preparation for useful activity after your retirement requires that you spend time to determine ahead just what things are worth pursuing. With a list of objectives not dominated by human selfishness you can welcome your retirement as a time in which you will be free to work at those useful activities in which you have accumulated some experience.

You can run to retirement or you can run from retirement. And the direction you are likely to take will depend to a large extent on what useful activities have occupied your attention. And that useful means useful to society.

To retire *from* is a real tragedy. To retire *to* can mark the beginning of the most satisfying part of your entire life. I've seen a happy retirement add zest to the very life of my friends. I've seen a sparkle in their eyes and the glow of good health in their cheeks.

The major scourges of modern man are not the result of poor diet, faulty hygiene, or excessive fatigue, but to a great extent to aimless living. When the zest for living is lost, you may find senility is almost inevitable.

In addition to maintaining energy through exercises for the body, the principal need of the older people is a specific motivation—a justification for living these added years. Since positive health is more than an absence of disease, the emotional drives, personal interest and sense of values all play a key role in your daily activities.

Learn at All Ages

The trouble with old age most people find is that while the body may not function as well as it did and your bones are more apt to feel the cold, the mind still keeps working at high speed. People are capable of learning at all ages.

At age 60, psychologists who have studied the problem say, full mental maturity is finally reached. The decline that does set in is still so slow that at the age of 80 we still have the learning ability of a 25-year-old. You can learn a foreign language, study nature, or learn of the magical worlds of music and art. Age is no barrier to taking up new interests and enjoying the pleasures of relaxed study. Age is no defense, therefore, against the feeling of defeat which can come from a feeling of being unwanted or unneeded.

Balanced Living

Finding a balanced way of living for a long life is not a difficult problem to solve. We need to face up to the things which block our way to finer living. Retirement has different meanings for different people. It matters chiefly what one retires to and what is in store for the future in terms of continued physical activity and satisfactory mental occupation. These factors should be studied in terms of long-range satisfactions of achievement and fulfillment.

I've heard it said that George Washington retired four times, the first time when he was only 28. Each time he became withdrawn and unhappy. He was cured by being called back into active service by his country. Benjamin Franklin retired from an everyday business life at the age of 40. As you know he lived a long and even more active and exciting life from that time on.

The Good Home Life

Ranking with your good health in importance to an enjoyable retirement is a good home life. While you are spending your days in the shop or at your office, you can usually stand the upsets at home without too much trouble. After you retire and the home becomes your full-time base of operations, the minor problems suddenly assume giant proportions.

Having a happy home life in retirement is not just a matter of getting along with your spouse. There are many other important factors. For example, what changes will you make in your living arrangements? What will your housing needs be? Should you move elsewhere? We'll take a closer look at this housing problem a bit later in this chapter.

Your close proximity twenty-four hours a day may subject your marriage to new strains after retirement. A husband and wife should work closely together now to plan for the later years of life. In this joint planning, try to take into full account the interests and desires of both of you. So many people evolve all their retirement plans around their own wishes and interests. They completely forget that their spouses also have the right to retire. On some points you will have to come up with a working compromise. But by knowing the possible differences in advance and having a loving regard for each other, you should be able to think of solutions that will be quite satisfactory for both of you.

Friends Are Necessary

One reason why many older people lose their interest in living is the lack of friends. They say they had friends once, but their friends passed on or moved away. What they are faced with is not so much the lack of friends, but the loss of friendliness. The secret of avoiding this friendless existence is to keep your interest in other people strong as you grow older. Do not let yourself be upset by the weaknesses or frailties of others.

While you are on the job, associates in your office or your industry take the place of friends to a very close degree. But once you retire, true friends are extremely necessary. The answer is to seek out and to cultivate new friends as you go along, never forgetting your old ones. Friendships do not just happen. They take cultivation and an outgoing effort.

Closely related to this problem of friendships is the problem about a place to live that was touched upon earlier. A major decison you must make is whether to move to a new community or to stay on in the old homestead. In discussing this problem with the personnel directors of companies, I've been told that perhaps half of all retirees would do well to move to another community. The other half will live quite happily in the old home town. It all depends on how much you have become attached to the old community and your neighbors.

One of the biggest reasons for moving to another area for some retirees is the change in their own neighborhood. There seems to be a definite pattern in neighborhood changes all over the country. Over a period of time the neighborhood changes from young marrieds soon with children, to a settled area with the youngsters growing up. While this is going on, some of the homes are being sold. Finally, when your own children are married and in homes of their own, you are apt to find most of the homes of your street occupied by a new influx of young marrieds, with youngsters who are apt to be annoying with their antics. Older people usually want a bit more quiet and are not that likely to remember how their own children acted. Some retirees soon acquire the reputation of crabs and their relations with the rest of their neighbors is often cold, sometimes bordering on open hostility. This is a major reason for considering a move. The other reason, of course, is that you probably no longer need the same space you did earlier.

Your Physical Well-Being

Ideally, a husband and wife should enjoy good health. You can help assure this for your later life by taking regular physical examinations and by living wholesome, moderate lives. Strangely enough, most men seem to undergo these examinations, but few ever think of having their wives examined. Chances are many women never have a physical after childbirth unless they become quite ill.

The information in Chapters 7 and 8 will be of assistance in helping you keep yourself in good shape.

If you are healthy, normally you'll be an optimistic, well-integrated personality who will be able to find new friends wherever you go. You can secure such a personality if you practice the art of getting along with others well in advance of retirement. Now, you'll have a basketful of things to help you occupy your time.

Retirement Income

To complete the retirement ideal, you'll have a comfortable income. Here again, you must secure this in advance by making financial plans well ahead of time.

Common sense tells you that your plans for retirement should include a plan for retirement income. The extent of this income depends on your ability to save or build resources for it, and, to some degree, on what you plan to do with your life after retiring.

In any event, the sooner you begin a regular savings program, the easier it will be for you. Not only will the necessary savings be spread over a longer period of time, but compounded interest will work more in your favor in reducing the effort you have to make to save sufficient money. This also means choosing plans that will provide the greatest returns throughout your life. An investment advisor is perhaps the best investment you can make.

What of Your Business?

Your business, if you are the owner, will be an important factor in your future. Carefully managed, it may be all you need for financial security at retirement. Badly managed, it might be a white elephant which could upset your retirement plans or timing. So prudence here is as important as it is in any of the other parts of your retirement program.

If you work for somebody else, a pension plan will be a good foundation for building financial security in later life. If your company does not believe in providing pension plans for its help, you face the task of carefully planning your own retirement program. This does not mean that you have to work in the dark. You will be able to gain a great deal of advice from your banker, your insurance agent, investment advisors, and similar counselors.

I suggest you sit down in a quiet spot and outline just what you now have working for you when you retire. Then discuss this important subject with your spouse to obtain his/her ideas. If you feel you need a broader program, don't hesitate to take immediate action—the sooner the better. Set up a timetable, stick to it, and enjoy your later life as an active, healthy and good citizen.

Throughout this book I've tried to offer guidelines that will help you toward greater success in both your business and personal lives. This problem of a happy retirement, and it is just as important a problem as any other I have discussed, can be solved by careful planning and self-management.

If you will but make the effort to manage yourself . . . you will have all the time you need to enjoy life to its fullest.